REFUGEES
The Time Travellers

REFUGEES
The Time Travellers

Susheel Gajwani

BLACK EAGLE BOOKS
Dublin, USA | Bhubaneswar, India

Black Eagle Books
USA address:
7464 Wisdom Lane
Dublin, OH 43016

India address:
E/312, Trident Galaxy, Kalinga Nagar,
Bhubaneswar-751003, Odisha, India

E-mail: info@blackeaglebooks.org
Website: www.blackeaglebooks.org

First International Edition Published by
Black Eagle Books, 2025

REFUGEES: THE TIME TRAVELLERS
by **Susheel Gajwani**

Copyright © **Susheel Gajwani & Neetu Gajwani**

All rights reserved. No part of this publication may be reproduced, stored in a retrieval system, or transmitted, in any form or by any means, electronic, mechanical, photocopying, recording or otherwise without the prior permission of the publisher.

Cover & Interior Design: Ezy's Publication

ISBN- 978-1-64560-766-3 (Paperback)

Printed in the United States of America

Dedicated to my grandparents

Paari Parchomal Gajwani
&
Parchomal Jadalmal Gajwani

Author's Note

Refugees – The Time Travellers

The journey of this book began long before I wrote its first line. It began in memories—some inherited, some discovered, and some recovered from the silences that history often leaves behind.

My earlier work, *Sunrise over Valivade*, grew out of my attempt to understand the lived realities of the Sindhi refugees who once inhabited the Valivade camp near Kolhapur. As I listened to stories, pored over documents, and absorbed the voices of those who had endured displacement, I realized that history is not a closed chapter. For many, it continues to breathe, ache, and guide. *Aakhreen Train – The Last Train*, my Sindhi film, further deepened this realization. While making it, I witnessed how trauma and resilience travel across generations—how the Partition, though decades behind us, shapes identities, relationships, and cultural memory even today.

My program *ROOTS – The Time Travellers*, based on Partition poetry in Sindhi, affirmed something profound: that refugees are not only carriers of loss but also custodians of language, culture, and wisdom. Poetry—written in the throes of separation—revealed how time bends for those who have lived through upheaval. They carry the past within them, even as they build new futures.

Refugees – The Time Travellers is born from this continuum.

This book is not merely about displacement; it is about movement through time—about how refugees navigate generations with memories that do not age, with stories that refuse to fade, and with hope that insists on surviving. Refugees are, in many ways, time travellers. They arrive in new lands carrying the echoes of old worlds; they shape histories while being shaped by them; they hold on to culture not as nostalgia but as a lifeline.

In writing this book, I have tried to honour those journeys. I have tried to capture not just the pain of leaving but the courage of starting again, the brilliance with which displaced communities recreate identity, and the quiet heroism that often goes unrecorded.

If *Sunrise over Valivade* illuminated one chapter, *Aakhreen Train* The Last Train dramatized another, and *ROOTS – The Time Travellers* explored the poetic soul of a people, then this book brings them all together. It is a remembrance, a tribute, and a bridge—connecting past and present, memory and imagination, loss and renewal.

My hope is that readers will not only learn about refugees but *feel* their journeys—feel the timelessness of their struggles, the endurance of their culture, and the extraordinary human spirit that transcends borders and eras.

For in telling their stories, we do not just revisit the past. We travel through time with them.

— **Susheel Gajwani**
Email- susheelgajwani@gmail.com

Acknowledgements

Refugees – The Time Travellers has taken shape through the love, encouragement, and steadfast faith of many cherished individuals. To each of you, I offer my deepest gratitude.

My first and most profound thanks go to my wife, Bharti, whose calm strength, quiet understanding, and unwavering support have carried me through every step of this journey. To my children, Neetu and Goldie, your affection, enthusiasm, and belief in my work have been a source of constant joy and inspiration. You have all held me up more than you know.

I owe a special debt of gratitude to my brother, the irrepressible and brilliant Shashi Gajwani—poet, lyricist, producer, and director—whose keen insight into the human heart has illuminated my path. His ability to see the story within the story, to recognise the soul of its characters, has enriched this book.

My friend Gyan Narsinghani who has been such a great support, no matter what.

My warm appreciation goes to the talented Barkha Khushalani, a poet, lyricist , writer. Your insistence on reaching further has pushed me gently yet firmly toward my best. And to Menka Shivdasani, a poet of rare grace, thank you for your kindness, support, and belief in my voice.

I am also grateful to Dr. Subhadra Anand for her thoughtful guidance and for suggesting the title, Refugees – The Time Travellers, for this book. Her insight added a dimension that resonates at the book's heart.

My heartfelt thanks extend as well to Black Eagle Books and its Founder- Director Satya Pattanaik, whose care, commitment, and refined aesthetic have given this work a home of true elegance. Their dedication to quality has brought the book into the world with dignity and style.

To all of you, I extend my sincerest thanks. Without your generosity, love, and unwavering belief, Refugees – The Time Travellers would never have found its voice—or its wings.

- **Susheel Gajwani**

Contents

1.	The Road of Fire	13
2.	The Sea between the Worlds	20
3.	The Song of the River	24
4.	Traders and Travellers	29
5.	The voyage	32
6.	The Lost City	34
7.	Camp of Dust and Hope	38
8.	The Woman who carried a Kingdom	43
9.	The River and the Sea	48
10.	The Market Place of Hope	52
11.	Valivade refugee camp	55
12.	The Shadow of Loss	60
13.	Embers beneath the Ashes	62
14.	Standing Tall	66
15.	The Bridge Builder	68
16.	Seven Miles to Kolhapur	72
17.	Poet of the Two Worlds	76
18.	The letter that found its way	85
19.	Polish Refugees in Valivade	91
20.	The Second World War	96
21.	Polish Boys Cycling to Goa	115
22.	The School with no Country	120
23.	Every night. At midnight	125
24.	The Polish Camp	130
25.	The night of no Fear	135
26.	Friendship and Fizz in Valivade	139
27.	The Line of Dust	144
28.	Midnight Rescue	150
29.	The Partition	156

To my wonderful parents

Bajomal Parchomal Gajwani &
Bhagyavanti Bajomal Gajwani

Chapter 1

The Road of Fire

The dusty road out of Shahdadkot, Larkana, shimmered under the unforgiving Sindh sun, the horizon stretching into a haze of uncertainty.

Bajo's heart pounded like a war drum as the small caravan trudged forward—ox carts creaking, bundles of meager belongings tied with frayed ropes, and frightened eyes darting in every direction.

The air was thick with the smell of fear and the dry scent of burning earth.

For centuries, their family had called Shahdadkot home.

Generations of love, harvest, business, laughter, and prayers lay buried in its soil.

Now, they fled it all—refugees on their own land — driven towards Karachi and the hope of boarding a ship to Bombay.

Bajo, seventeen, walked at the front.

He carried his father's old knife, not meant for violence but for self-defence.

Beside him strode Anand, his younger brother, fierce-eyed and barely fifteen.

Behind them were their neighbours—Bansi, always the quickest with a joke but now silent as stone; their parents Paari and Parchomal; grandparents Bakhat and Jaadalmal, and a handful of others—mothers, infants, and elders, all weighed down by grief and dread.

Paari, her hair silver as moonlight, clutched prayer beads and whispered mantras under her breath.

Parchomal, his face like carved wood, carried nothing but a walking stick and the weight of an ancestral promise: protect the family, no matter the cost.

Then the stillness shattered.

A chilling cry echoed over the arid plain.

Hooves pounded like thunder.

Dark figures emerged from the horizon—men wild-eyed and snarling, weapons glinting in the ruthless sun.

The Muhajirs.

Bajo's breath caught in his throat. "Anand! Look into their eyes!" Chaos erupted.

Swords clanged, fists flew.

Bajo met the first attacker head-on, his knife deflecting a blow by sheer instinct.

Anand struck wildly with an iron rod, his boyish face twisted in raw fury.

Bansi tackled a bandit, rolling in the dust. "Get the women out!" Parchomal roared, swinging his stick with surprising force.

Paari, her hands trembling, pulled a sobbing child towards the carts.

A blow sent Bajo sprawling.

Pain flared in his shoulder.

Blood darkened his shirt.

He staggered upright, heart screaming, vision blurred.

And amid the maelstrom, Bajo's wife fifteen year old Bhagyavanti was on her toes.

She had been quiet through most of the journey,

thoughtful eyes watching, mind racing.

Now she moved with sudden clarity.

She reached the overturned cart where her youngest cousin wailed beneath splintered wood. "Bakhat Ma! We need fire!" Grandmother Bakhat—in her 60's but fierce in spirit—nodded. "Smoke.

Horses hate smoke." Bhagyavanti tore strips of cloth. Bakhat, steady despite her shaking limbs, lit the fabric with embers from a shattered clay stove.

Flames flickered.

Smoke billowed. "Set the grain sacks ablaze!" Bhagyavanti ordered. "Quickly!" The plan worked.

The attackers' horses panicked, rearing and whinnying in terror.

Confusion spread through the ranks of the Muhajirs.

Faces masked in fear.

Movement slowed.

In that breath of opportunity, Anand struck down his assailant.

Bajo, limping, heaved his wounded brother back to his feet.

Parchomal bellowed invocations to Guru NanakDev, his voice hoarse but unbroken.

Paari pulled two children close, her chants rising above the din.

Bhagyavanti and Bakhat shepherded the others— mothers, toddlers, wounded men— towards the side path leading to the riverbank.

Bansi, bloodied and gasping, covered the retreat, eyes scanning wildly for any straggler.

Only when the smoke choked the sky and the sounds of pursuit faded did they pause.

The survivors collapsed—panting, bruised, alive.

Bajo dropped to his knees, his hands shaking uncontrollably.

Anand sat beside him, tears tracking down dust-streaked cheeks.

Paari pressed her forehead to Parchomal's chest, silent sobs wracking her frame.

Bhagyavanti sat on the ground, her breath slow but steady, hands still soot-blackened.

Beside her, Bakhat closed her eyes, lips murmuring prayers that stretched back beyond memory.

The road to Karachi still lay long and perilous.

But they had survived the worst.

The caravan, battered but not broken, rose again under the crimson Sindhi sky.

And ahead—far ahead—the salt air of Karachi whispered of ships, of oceans, of new beginnings.

And of home, somewhere beyond the flames.

The moon hung like a pale coin in the ink-black sky as Bajo and his family trudged through the brittle wilderness.

Every step felt heavier than the last.

The distant echo of their earlier battle still rang in their ears—phantom sounds of hooves, shouts, the clash of metal.

They were alive, but the price had been dear.

Three young men killed, two oxen were lost, supplies scattered, and several among them bore wounds both seen and unseen.

Yet the road stretched on, and with it, the fragile thread of hope.

Parchomal limped, his hand clutched to his ribs, Paari steadying him.

Anand refused to be carried despite the gash on his leg.

Bansi, his face bloodied and swollen, scouted ahead with watchful eyes.

Bhagyavanti and Bakhat moved quietly among the group, tending to the injured, murmuring comfort to children who clung to their mothers.

Bajo carried his youngest cousin in his arms.

The child's tears had dried hours ago, exhaustion overtaking fear.

Each time Bajo's knees threatened to buckle, he remembered his father's voice: "The strongest shoulders carry the weakest hearts." They camped in a hollow under a twisted neem tree.

The night air was sharp, the desert wind whispering secrets of the anciet times.

They lit no fire—only cold phulkas passed from hand to hand, water shared sparingly.

The silence was broken only by the soft hum of Paari's lullabies—half prayer, half song.

Bhagyavanti sat apart, her eyes fixed on the stars.

Bakhat settled beside her brave daughter-in-law, wrapping the shawl tighter around her frail form. "Do you remember the story of Mai Kolachi?" Bakhat whispered.

Bhagyavanti nodded. "The woman who founded Karachi." "She braved storms and the sea to save her people," Bakhat said softly. "You have her courage.

We all do." Tears prickled Bhagyavanti's eyes, but she held them back. "We have to make it.

For them." By dawn, they moved again, the bruised sky softening to gold.

They reached the dusty outskirts of Larkana and found temporary refuge in a shrine.

The caretakers—a Sufi elder and his family—shared what little food they had.

But time pressed on.

Rumours of roadblocks, of mobs closing routes reached them.

The final stretch to Karachi would be the hardest.

Late that night, as the caravan prepared for the final push, Bajo gathered Anand, Bansi, Bhagyavanti, and Bakhat. "We cannot take the main road," Bajo said. "We'll follow the old river path.

It's longer, but safer." Anand, pale but defiant, nodded.

Bansi tightened his grip on a salvaged spear.

Bhagyavanti's eyes shone in the moonlight.

They moved in silence—ghosts in the darkness.

Hours blurred into one another.

Somewhere beyond the horizon, the first scent of sea air touched their senses.

Karachi was close.

But so was danger.

As they crossed a narrow gorge, shadows stirred.

Another ambush.

This time, fewer Muhajirs—but no less lethal.

The group scattered.

Bansi fought hand-to-hand, Anand shielded Paari and Parchomal.

Bajo flung himself between the attackers and Bhagyavanti.

It was Bhagyavanti, however, who saved them again.

From her satchel, she pulled fistfuls of red chillies—the last of their supplies—and hurled them onto the attackers' torches.

Flames and choking smoke blinded the Muhajirs.

Bakhat raised her arms and wailed a chant that seemed to shatter the night itself.

The attackers broke.
The family fled.
And at last—just as dawn painted the sky in pink and gold—they crested a hill and saw it: The sea.
The ships.
Karachi.
Bajo sank to his knees.
Anand laughed, a sound choked with tears.
Bhagyavanti covered her mouth in disbelief.
They had made it.
For now.
The road to Bombay—and the unknown future—lay ahead.

Chapter 2

The Sea between the Worlds

The ship creaked like an ancient creature burdened with too many souls.

Its wooden hull groaned as it heaved through the dark waters of the Arabian Sea, carrying hundreds of refugees from Sindh—each with a bundle of possessions, a clutch of memories, and a wound that had no bandage.

Bajo stood at the rail, the salt wind biting his face.

The air smelled of sweat, brine, and despair.

Around him, families huddled beneath shawls, whispering prayers into the endless night.

Somewhere below deck, a child whimpered for water.

The ship's engine coughed and sputtered like a dying animal.

He closed his eyes, the roar of the waves echoing the thunder in his chest.

Behind him, Bhagyavanti moved quietly, her hands full of clay cups filled with what little tea she'd managed to barter from a sailor.

Her face glowed faintly in the lantern light—exhausted, soot-streaked, and yet calm in a way that stilled something in him. "Drink," she said softly, offering him a cup.

He took it, their fingers brushing.

The touch was brief but grounding, a reminder that they were still here—still human—amid the storm of exile.

Below deck, Paari tended to Parchomal.

He lay propped against a sack of grain, his breathing ragged.

The wound on his ribs had festered despite Bhagyavanti's care.

Paari's fingers trembled as she wiped his forehead with the corner of her dupatta.

"Rest," she whispered.

"Bombay is close.

Parchomal's eyes flickered open.

"Closer than we were," he murmured, a shadow of a smile tugging at his cracked lips.

"And farther from what we were." Paari turned away before he could see her tears.

On the other side, Bakhat sat wrapped in her old shawl, her spine bent but her gaze fierce.

Jadalmal, her husband, leaned beside her, silent as the sea.

He hadn't spoken much since they left Shahdadkot.

Words, it seemed, had no meaning after you had watched your home vanish in fire and dust.

But tonight, as the ship rocked, he reached for Bakhat's hand.

"Do you remember," he said, his voice hoarse, "the first time we saw the Sindhu in flood?

The whole world appeared golden.

The air smelled of rain and mustard." Bakhat nodded slowly.

"And the children ran barefoot through the fields.

Anand had caught a fish with his hands.

Bajo climbed the neem tree and refused to come down." Her eyes glistened.

"That was before all this." "Yes," Jadalmal said.

"Before." Above them, the sea rose like a breathing thing.

A storm had been building since sunset.

Now the wind lashed the deck, flinging salt spray into the faces of those who clung to the railing.

Mothers tightened their arms around infants; men braced themselves against the railings.

The cries of the sick and frightened merged with the hiss of the waves.

Bajo felt the ship tilt sharply.

A shout went up—"Hold fast!"—and the deck seemed to spin.

Bhagyavanti grabbed his arm, steadying him.

The clay cup shattered at their feet, spilling its contents into the sea.

"Below!" someone yelled.

"Everyone below!" But there was no room below.

The decks were packed, every inch taken by the desperate and displaced.

Bajo shielded Bhagyavanti with his body as a wave crashed over them, soaking them to the bone.

"Hold on!" he shouted, gripping the rail.

Lightning split the sky—a white wound across blackness.

For a moment, the sea was illuminated: the waves like walls of glass, the ship a fragile dot between their fury, Bhagyavanti's hair whipped around her face, and she screamed something—he couldn't hear it—but her eyes burned with the same fire that had saved them on the road.

Then, just as suddenly, the storm broke.

The wind eased.

The waves sank back into uneasy rhythm.

The ship drifted forward, battered but alive.

Paari joined Bajo and her daughter-in-law Bhagyavanti.

Watching the sea waves, Bajo recalled the river Sindhu and the time he spent with his mother Paari on its banks.

Chapter 3

The Song of the River

The Sindhu River flows silver under the afternoon sun. The breeze carries the scent of wet earth, cumin, and the distant sound of children's laughter.

Paari Amma and her son, sixteen-year-old Bajo, walk barefoot along the riverbank, feeling the pulse of history beneath their feet.

Bajo (eyes bright, looking out over the water): Amma… I feel it.

The strength.

The river never forgets.

It remembers who we are… who we were… and who we can be.

Amma (softly, reverent, proud): Yes, my son.

We are not just walking along a river.

We are walking on history.

On civilizations.

On Mooenjo-Daro, on the dreams of our ancestors who built wide streets, precise bricks, the Great Bath — the first temple of cleanliness.

Democracy and justice… carved into geometry, even before the world knew the words.

Bajo (voice filled with wonder): Amma… it feels alive.

Like it's teaching us… like the river itself is speaking.

Amma (nodding, lyrical, voice strong): Yes, Putra.

I am joy.

I am celebration.

I am Marui dancing in the deserts of Thar, refusing kings.

I am the dervishes spinning in Sehwan, laughing with devotion.

I am the women of Sindh, rising with song in one hand, knowledge in the other, courage in the heart.

True love, true longing—lit the lamps of the soul." — Shah Abdul Latif Bhittai Even when empires faded, even when the river turned.

Even when the world tried to forget us... we survived.

We sang.

We traded.

We welcomed the traveller.

Bajo (pointing to the horizon, excited): Amma... the children, the music, the laughter... it's all part of us.

All part of Sindh.

Amma (voice rising, inspiring): Exactly, Bajo.

This is modernity from ancient times.

This is courage, generosity, and joy.

This is the Sindh that gave birth to poets, mystics, traders, lovers... not conquerors.

The wind carries the tamburo's melody from a distant shrine.

Children's laughter echoes from the fields.

Ajrak patterns sway in the breeze.

The scent of cumin, of wet soil, of possibility fills the air.

Amma (kneeling, touching the earth, solemn and joyful): We are Sindh.

We are alive.

We are here.

In the river.

In the soil.

In the music.

In the stories.

In the laughter.

In the courage of every woman, every child, every poet, every traveller who ever called this home.

"Let it happen if it must.

If not, then let it go.

But the breath of those beloved ones never fades." — Shah Abdul Latif Bhittai

Bajo (taking Amma's hand, inspired): We will carry it forward, Amma.

Everywhere.

Let the world see... Sindh is alive.

Sindh is ours.

Amma (raising her hand to the sky): Yes, my son.

Tell them, when they ask, "Who built the first song? The first rhythm of the East?"

Bajo (strong, clear): Not Greece.

Not Rome.

Not Babylon.

Amma and Bajo (together, ringing with pride and joy): Tell them: Sindh.

The river glows gold as the sun dips toward the horizon.

The song of the river, of the land, of generations — continues, eternal, joyful, unbroken.

"You are the light, the body, the soul — you are everything." — Shah Abdul Latif Bhittai.

The sun has sunk low, leaving the Sindhu in hues of amber and bronze.

Bajo and Amma walk along the riverbank until the song of the water fades into the quiet hum of evening.

Ahead rise the ruins of a city — Mooenjo-Daro,

shimmering faintly in the last light.

Bajo (softly, awe in his voice): Amma... is this where it began?

Amma (her voice like wind over stone): Yes, my son.

Here they built the first dream — of balance, of beauty, of belonging.

Before pyramids rose on the Nile, before laws echoed in Babylon, before Athens thought itself wise — Sindh was already thinking, already living.

They step into the ruins.

The wind stirs the dust, lifting echoes of footsteps long gone.

The air smells faintly of baked clay and old rain.

Amma (touching a crumbling wall): These bricks once held laughter, arguments, prayers.

Each one measured with care — not by slaves, but by equals.

Here, water ran through streets clean as conscience.

Here, the Great Bath was built — not for kings, but for all.

Bajo (troubled): Then why does it lie silent now, Amma?

Amma (pausing): Because wisdom can turn to pride... and pride forgets its purpose.

When the heart grows blind, even order becomes a cage.

When compassion dries, even rivers change their course.

Bajo kneels beside a broken seal — a tiny carving of a bull, proud and silent.

Bajo (holding the seal reverently): Their stories are still here — written in silence.

Amma (smiling): Silence is also a language, my son.

One only the humble can hear.

They walk deeper into the ruins.

For a moment, Bajo sees flickers — artisans carving seals, children playing by wells, a scholar drawing lines on a tablet.

The city breathes again, alive, rhythmic, glowing in its simplicity.

Bajo (whispering): They were just like us... dreaming, building, loving.

Amma (softly): Perhaps they built knowing that nothing lasts — except the idea.

And the idea was this: To live not above the earth, but with it.

To rule not with the hand, but with the heart.

The wind rises, scattering dust into the dying light.

Bajo (kneeling, pressing his palm into the soil): Let this dust remember us, Amma — as we remember them.

Chapter 4

Traders and Travellers

Morning breaks over the desert like a golden hymn.
Bajo and Amma walk side by side.

Ahead, camels sway in rhythm; traders, mystics, and travellers from Persia, Arabia, and China join the path.

The air hums with languages older than memory.

Caravan Leader (greeting them): Peace be upon you, travellers of the river.

Amma (bowing): Peace be upon you, too, brother.

Toward Sehwan, where the saints still dance. As they move together, the desert teaches patience, humility, and listening.

Persian poets, Chinese monks, Arab traders — all share wisdom, music, and stories.

Bajo begins to hear Sindh's song in every voice.

Bajo (quietly): Amma… are we merchants too, then? Saudagar?

Amma (smiling): Yes, my son — but not only of things.

We trade in kindness.

Our coin is compassion; our goods are understanding.

Night falls.

Around the campfire, languages blend in a beautiful medley of sound.

Bajo begins to feel the rhythm of Sindh inside himself — alive, eternal, unbroken.

The caravan reaches Sehwan.

Amma and Bajo on a camel, too.

The shrine of Lal Shahbaz Qalandar hums with drums, chants, and spinning devotees.

The air trembles with joy and devotion.

Bajo (awe-struck): Amma, are they praying or celebrating?

Amma (smiling): Both.

In Sindh, prayer is celebration — and celebration is surrender.

Bajo steps into the circle.

The drumbeat merges with his heartbeat.

He spins, dissolving into rhythm, into the same energy that carried the river, Mooenjo-Daro, and the ancient poets.

He experiences transcendence.

Bajo (whispering): Then to dance… is to remember.

Amma: Yes, Putra, to remember that we are one.

One breath, one river, one love.

As night deepens, the drums fade into a steady pulse — like the river breathing beneath the earth.

A few months later, Bajo walks in Karachi's harbor.

The sea roars, the city hums — horns, engines, voices.

He watches a young artist painting the river on a wall.

Bajo: That river… you've painted her memory.

Do you know her song?

Artist: No one remembers the words anymore.

But the rhythm — it still finds us.

Bajo realizes the song of Sindh survives — in art, compassion, and memory.

Rain begins to fall, washing the city in silver.

He raises his arms to the sky.

Bajo: Sindh — I hear you!

In engines, in markets, in rain on concrete!

You are alive — in us, through us, still!

The storm subsides.

The city glows anew — restless, alive, carrying the river's unbroken melody.

Bajo returns to the Sindhu River.

He kneels, letting cold water run over his palms.

His notebook rests nearby — filled with poetry, sketches, and fragments of the city's rhythm.

This is the story of Sindh...

Bajo (softly): Amma... the river kept its promise.

Even when I could not.

The young artist from Karachi joins him.

He opens his notebook and begins writing aloud: We are the song between water and wind.

We are not lost — only louder now.

This is the story of Sindh — where the first brick met the first poem, where dust dreamed itself into dawn." The wind rises, carrying his voice across the water.

Stars shimmer overhead.

Bajo: "The Song of the River." It began here.

It ends here.

And it will begin again. "The river flows, but the song remains." — Bhittai.

Chapter 5

The voyage

Bajo is awakened from his memories by his wife Bhagyavanti

He looks at her and smiles.

Hours later, a pale dawn crept across the horizon.

Bajo and Bhagyavanti sat together near the bow, wrapped in a shared blanket, trembling from cold and exhaustion.

Behind them, Paari dozed against Parchomal's shoulder.

His breathing had steadied.

Bakhat and Jadalmal murmured prayers to the rising sun, voices soft but unbroken.

"Three days," Bhagyavanti whispered.

"They said it would be three days." Bajo nodded.

"Then Bombay." She looked out at the endless expanse of water.

"Do you think it will feel like home?" He was silent for a long moment.

"Maybe not.

But it will be where we begin again." The ship rocked gently beneath them.

Around them, the refugees began to stir—some weeping quietly, some murmuring morning prayers.

The sun lifted higher, gilding the sea with gold.

For the first time in months, the light felt warm instead of cruel.

By afternoon, the sailors began to shout.

"Land!

Land ahead!" A cry spread across the decks, swelling like a tide.

People rushed to the rails, straining to see.

And there it was—faint, shimmering, but real—the hazy outline of Bombay rising from the sea.

Paari clasped Parchomal's hand.

Bakhat whispered a prayer of thanks.

Bhagyavanti pressed her palms together and closed her eyes.

Bajo simply stared, the wind drying the tears he hadn't realized he'd shed.

Behind them, the sea whispered and sighed, carrying away the ghosts of Shahdadkot.

Larkana.

Ahead, the new world awaited—crowded, uncertain, but alive.

And as the ship glided toward the harbour, Bajo reached for Bhagyavanti's hand.

This time, she didn't let go.

The voyage had ended.

The journey had only begun.

Chapter 6

The Lost City

The Railway, the Bricks, the Lost City—and the People. At dawn, the city awakens.

A potter stirs his kiln, lifting freshly fired bricks with care.

Children splash in the bath at the corner well.

Merchants weigh grain in the bazaar, their seals pressed with bulls and elephants.

Water runs through covered drains, clean and steady, carrying away the night.

The city breathes in rhythm with the Indus.

Four thousand five hundred years later, another dawn breaks.

This time in Valivade, in a refugee camp outside Kolhapur.

Children cry in the milk queue, their ribs showing through tattered shirts.

Mothers clutch empty vessels, waiting, waiting.

Grandmothers tell stories—not of the houses left behind in Sindh, but of a city older still, a city where their ancestors built with the same bricks now stolen for railway tracks.

Mooenjo-Daro.

Mound of the Dead.

Mound of the Living, too, for it beats inside their chest.

The streets of Larkana and the lanes of the camp blur into one another.
One city buried by silt, another buried by Partition.
Both enduring in silence.
Both waiting for rediscovery.
The British railway project in India began in the 1850s. The first train ran between Bombay and Thane in 1853. By the late 1850s, engineers were already laying tracks in Punjab and Sindh.
In the absence of cheap kiln-fired bricks, they turned to the ancient mounds at Harappa and Mooenjo-Daro.
John Marshall, Director-General of the Archaeological Survey of India, later lamented: "The greater part of the ruined site was destroyed by the railway contractors, who carried away the bricks by the cartload for ballast." Entire walls, drains, and courtyards of Harappa and Mooenjo-Daro disappeared beneath the steel of the Lahore–Multan line.
Only decades later would archaeologists pause to look deeper.
In 1921, Daya Ram Sahni began systematic excavations at Harappa.
In 1922, Rakhaldas Banerji investigated a mound near Larkana.
At first, he thought it was a Buddhist stupa.
But within months, his trenches revealed streets of baked brick and seals inscribed with strange signs.
By 1924, Marshall announced to the world that India's history stretched back to the Indus Valley Civilization, as old as Egypt and Mesopotamia.
Mooenjo-Daro revealed a city of 40,000–50,000 people: carefully planned streets, two-storey houses, private wells, covered drainage, the Great Bath, and standardized brickwork.

It was a revelation — and for Sindh, a source of pride. But history turned.

In 1947, Partition uprooted more than a million Sindhi Hindus and Sikhs.

They crossed from Sindh into other parts of India as refugees in their own country, leaving Sindh behind forever.

For them, Mooenjo-Daro was more than ruins.

It was a portable homeland.

Refugee poets and writers drew directly upon its symbolism.

One refugee wrote bitterly: "I have lost all of Sindh." The other demanded "Put in my claim for property, you say?

I claim the whole of Sind!" Another offered resilience: "Wherever you find Sindhis, call it your Sindh." A poet compared his people to a hardy tree: "Babool grows in any season...

Is it not a Sindhi?" Their imagery drew strength from Mooenjo-Daro itself: buried but not erased, silent but enduring.

Susheel Gajwani's memoir Sunrise Over Valivade captures this intersection of ancient pride and modern exile.

His family lived in the Valivade refugee camp on the outskirts of Kolhapur — once used by the Polish refugees during World War II.

He recalls: "Mothers and grandmothers have brought their little ones – a ragged, squalling lot, some naked – the words and the descriptions bring alive much more than the wretched, forlorn existence..." He remembers humiliation: "That word, Nirvashya [homeless, alien]... never failed to make me feel disgraced." And yet he remembers resilience too: the magnanimous Maharaja of Kolhapur personally welcoming Sindhi refugees with a hot meal on their arrival, and his grandmother Paari turning sorrow into laughter.

Valivade, like Mooenjo-Daro, became a paradox — a ruin that still contained life.

The bricks of Mooenjo-Daro once paved streets, later ballasted railways, and finally became symbols in exile.

Sindhis built new lives in India with those bricks of memory — language, food, poetry, prayer, and above all resilience.

As a young Sindhi later declared: "If Bharat is my mother, then Sindh is my grandmother...

Sindh and Sindhi is alive in me and it is immortal." The story of Sindhi refugees thus cannot be told apart from the story of Mooenjo-Daro.

Both were buried.

Both endured.

Both were rediscovered.

When refugees told tales of Mooenjo-Daro, it wasn't merely archaeology—they were invoking their roots, their pride.

Sindhi poets made these sentiments sing.

Lekhraj Aziz demanded sovereignty with lines like: "I claim the whole of Sind!"

Even in legal discourse, Mooenjo-Daro helped anchor identity.

Representing refugees, the distinguished lawyer Ram Jethmalani argued: "Sindh is not a piece of territory—it has its own civilisation..." The archaeological marvel of Mooenjo-Daro is engraved in deeply human experiences.

It becomes not just a relic of ancient civilization, but an emblem of a scattered people's undying connection to their roots.

Chapter 7

The Camp of Dust and Hope

The ship that had carried them across the sea now seemed like a distant dream.

Bombay —Alexandra Docks—was a crush of humanity, a maze of despair.

The air reeked of salt, oil, sweat, and sorrow.

Families huddled under canvas roofs or broken crates, their bundles stacked like tombstones of the lives they'd left behind.

Children cried for milk, old men for air.

For Bajo and Anand, the days blurred into hunger and noise.

Their father, Parchomal, had grown weak, the wound on his ribs refusing to heal in the damp dock air.

Paari tended to him.

The brothers had no money, only their will.

One morning, Bajo scavenged a broken basket from the dockside, patched it with jute ropes, and filled it with a dozen bananas he managed to buy on credit.

They walked to the crowded Victoria Terminus, where trains shrieked and human rivers surged through stone arches.

Bajo sat on the pavement, basket before him.

Passersby swept past without a glance.

The city was too busy for two Sindhi boys selling fruit.

Then Anand, always the clever one, had an idea.

He walked away into the crowd, then came back pretending to be a customer.

"Two bananas, bhai?" he said loudly, dropping a single paisa into Bajo's hand.

He peeled the fruit, ate it with exaggerated delight.

"Sweetest bananas in Bombay!" Heads turned.

A few curious men paused.

A porter bought one, then another man.

Soon the basket was half-empty.

Bajo looked up at Anand with something like pride in his tired eyes.

That night, they brought home six annas.

Enough for phulkas and a few vegetables.

Not enough for comfort—but enough for hope.

After a few days, the government officers came.

They called names from lists, shouted in Hindi and English.

Families were gathered in groups, told to pack quickly.

"You are being moved to camps," they said.

"Better food, better shelter." The Sindhi refugees climbed onto trains—wooden carriages meant for cattle, now packed with souls.

The train lurched and rattled out of Bombay, carrying three thousand men, women, and children toward the unknown.

From Bombay to Poona, then Poona to Miraj on a steam engine train, and from Miraj to Kolhapur in a passenger train on the narrow metre gauge line.

The steam engine screamed through the night, sparks flying from its iron wheels.

The refugees sat in silence, the rhythm of the wheels echoing the beat of their uncertainty.

Children slept in laps, heads against windows streaked with soot.

Mothers whispered prayers into the darkness.

From Miraj, they boarded the train on a narrow metre-gauge line—small, cramped, swaying as it wound through the fields.

The names of stations passed like a chant: Jaysingpur… Hathkangangale…

Rukadi…

Valivade Halt.

At Valivade, the train screeched to a halt.

The refugees poured out onto the dusty platform — thin, weary, clutching bundles and infants.

Ahead lay the Valivade Camp: rows upon rows of barracks, burning under the relentless Kolhapur sun.

The earth was cracked and red.

The air smelled of mud and sweat.

Yet, it was safety.

Government officers, aided by policemen, began calling out family names.

Confusion reigned.

Voices rose, tempers flared.

Some families were separated, others argued for space.

In the midst of the chaos, Bajo stepped forward.

"Let me help," he said.

He spoke calmly, communicating between officers and families.

He arranged lines, helped the elders find shade, guided mothers to the water spouts.

The officers, surprised by his composure, let him assist.

Slowly, order returned.

By nightfall, everyone had a roof— however humble—over their heads.

Paari wept when she saw their allotted barrack: a two room block, brick walls, and a floor made of old tiles.

"After all we've lost," she said, "even this feels like grace." Parchomal, though weak, nodded.

"A roof is a promise.

The rest we will build." The days in Valivade were harsh.

The monsoon turned the camp to red mud.

Food came in rations—grain, daal, a little oil.

Disease prowled among the children.

But the Sindhis were not the ones to surrender.

Each morning, the camp awoke to the sound of prayers and hammers.

Women formed sewing circles, mending clothes.

Men gathered, discussing business ideas, anything to regain dignity.

One man began frying pakoras; another carved combs from wood.

Bajo, restless and determined, gathered a small group—Anand, Bansi, Lolu and two other young men.

"We will not depend on charity," he said.

"We need work—trade.

Something of our own." Within weeks, their barrack, once bare, buzzed with activity.

Outside, the camp still smelled of heat and dust.

But within, something had changed.

Hope, like the small lamps they lit each night, burned stubbornly against the darkness.

And though the refugees of Valivade had lost their homeland, they began to find something else—a way to live again, with courage, with work, with dignity.

The Sindhi spirit, tested by fire, refused to break.

It only learned to bend—and rise.

Chapter 8

The Woman who carried a Kingdom

I was too young to understand Partition, too young to understand loss or borders or governments.

But I understood milk.

I understood the ache in my empty stomach.

And I understood the fear in the eyes of hundreds of children just like me—refugees who had fled from Sindh with nothing but their names, their gods, and the memory of a homeland that no longer belonged to them.

We stood in a serpentine queue outside the government milk-distribution centre in Valiwade Camp, Kolhapur.

Our families had been living there since 1950, thousands of Sindhi refugees in cramped barracks, trying to stitch new lives onto torn histories.

The walls of the centre were only mats of woven straw.

The roof was clay tiles.

Inside, a battered aluminum vessel held the only luxury our camp children knew—free milk from the government's relief programme.

The queue of children stretched endlessly—bare feet, dust-covered knees, bony shoulders.

Some wore ragged shorts; many had worn faded clothes.

But their eyes... their eyes shone with a hunger sharper than any wound.

They all watched the vessel as if it held a magic wand.

Each time the tumbler dipped, their eyes dipped.

Each time it rose, their eyes rose.

That was the rhythm of our morning—hope up, hope down.

A khaki-uniformed man poured milk with mechanical precision, as if he couldnt afford kindness.

Another washed glasses in a single bucket of water that smelled of metal and desperation.

Around us, the camp hummed with chaos— children screaming "kheer khape! kheer khape!

Want milk.

Want milk" Mothers in salwar-kameezes spoke in Sindhi, their words rising and falling like old folk songs, frayed but unbroken.

Some coaxed their children; others scolded them sharply.

But amidst all that noise, Paari stood like a rock.

My grandmother, Paari—her back straight, her chin high, her silver nose-ring flashing like a tiny sword.

Even in this situation, she dressed neatly, her dupatta pinned firmly, her hair oiled and tied.

She always said, "We lost our homes, not our honour." She placed me in the queue and kept her eyes on me, though she was talking to Nanki from Barrack 16.

I searched for her often, needing her presence like air.

Every time, I found the glint of her nose-ring, steady as a lighthouse.

I counted glasses greedily—one, two, three, four— each one a world of nourishment I longed to claim.

Just three children ahead of me now.

Then the sound I dreaded—the vessel scraping empty.

The younger children whimpered.

Older ones stared, frozen with fear.

But the glass-washer quickly mixed milk powder with water—this watery mixture was the taste of refugee life.

The foam rose brilliantly white, deceiving in its richness.

When my turn finally came, Paari stepped beside me.

Just then—everything froze.

The khaki man's hand stopped mid-air, the tumbler hovering above the glass.

His eyes dragged over me from my feet to my face, calculating, judging.

Then he barked, "Take this boy out.

Babya!

Hyaalaa baaher kaadh!" Babya, the glass-washer, grabbed my arm roughly and yanked me from the queue.

The world spun.

But Paari—Paari did not spin.

She stormed forward with the force of a monsoon wind.

"What are you doing?" She demanded.

"He is above the age limit," the man snapped.

Paari's nostrils flared.

"Who says so?" "I say.

Grown boys do not get milk."

"You call my child grown?" Her voice shook the air.

"He is not even four!

Are your eyes so blind?" "I know his age," he insisted.

Paari stepped even closer, her face inches from his.

"You?

You know the age of my grandchild?
Were you there when he was born?
When his mother gave him birth here in this camp?
You know?" The crowd fell silent.

The man, irritated, muttered, "These people... they'll do anything for free things." Paari's voice cracked like a whip.

"Free?

You think we stand here for charity?

You think refugees are beggars?

We lost our nation—not our pride." Her words pulsed with the weight of the Partition—of trains stained with blood, of nights spent fleeing, of elders left behind in burning cities.

She was not a woman who would be humiliated again.

Babya whispered, "Let the boy drink, baba... It's only milk." But the khaki man puffed up.

"I'm doing my duty."

"Your duty?" Paari scoffed.

"Your duty is to starve a refugee child?" Babya, angered, dipped a glass boldly into the vessel, filled it to the brim, and handed it to me.

The man froze, stunned.

I lifted the glass toward my lips—my first sip of hope—But suddenly Paari's hand, strong as iron, seized it.

Her voice boomed: " We do not drink from hands that insult us." And before anyone could breathe, she flung the milk into the man's face.

The white liquid splattered across his shirt like a slap from fate itself.

The glass smashed onto the ground, rolling away, its sound echoing through the straw-mat walls.

Paari grabbed my wrist and walked away—not hurriedly, not fearfully.

She walked like a queen majestically leaving an undeserving court.

And then, something miraculous happened.

One by one, the other mothers lifted their children from the queue.

They followed her silently—heads high, steps firm.

A river of dignity flowing behind a single resolute woman.

The khaki man stood frozen, milk dripping down his face, powerless before the storm that Paari had unleashed.

Babya cast an unhappy glance at the khaki man, and then, looked at the women walking away- with empathy.

This was Valiwade—the Sindhi refugee camp where thousands rebuilt their lives from dust and memories.

But on that day, I learned this: A homeland can be snatched.

A house can burn.

But as long as a woman like Paari stands her ground, a people's pride will never die.

Chapter 9

The River and the Sea

Long before Bajo was born, before the smoke of burning homes rose over Sindh, the land itself had been a crossing of worlds.

It was here that the Sindhu River met the Arabian Sea, and the tides carried stories farther than anyone could walk.

Paari used to say the river had memory.

She said it remembered the hands that shaped clay jars in Mooenjo-Daro, the traders who loaded lapis, cotton, and carnelian beads onto boats bound west.

Those boats, she said, were the first Sindhis to travel without fear.

In her telling, the ships pushed off from the delta at dawn, their sails catching the monsoon wind.

They followed the curve of the coast—Balakot, Sutkagen Dor, Lothal—then out across the open sea to Magan and Dilmun, and finally to Mesopotamia, where the Euphrates waited like a cousin of the Sindhu.

There, Sindhi traders set out their goods in sunbaked markets and were known by a single word the scribes wrote on clay: "Meluhha." "Meluhha was us," Paari would whisper.

"We traded not just wares, but trust.

Our forefathers' word was worth more than their gold." Sometimes Bajo imagined one of those merchants—

perhaps his own ancestor—standing on the deck of a creaking ship.

The sky wide, the sea endless, a brass diya burning by the mast to guide them home.

When storms rose, they held the lamp tight, never letting the flame die.

"Because," Paari would say, "light belongs to those who protect it." Now, as Bajo's bus rumbled toward Valivade, he thought of that river.

It did not stop at borders; it carved its own path through rock and sand, joined the sea, and kept moving.

So too had his family—forced to flow, yet never to vanish.

That evening in the refugee camp, Paari placed her brass diya on a tin trunk.

Its flame trembled in the dusty air, and she began to hum an old Sindhi tune—slow, steady, defiant.

"The river flows, the river remembers.

The river gives, and the river returns." The children listened wide-eyed.

For a moment, the barracks were not a camp but a harbour.

The soup in their bowls tasted of sea salt and home.

Paari turned to Bajo.

"Remember this, Bajo.

We come from traders, sailors, builders.

Our people crossed deserts and seas with their heads held high.

Even in exile, we do not lose that blood.

Wherever the river carries us, we will make the banks bloom again." Bajo nodded, feeling something old awaken inside him—a pride older than borders, stronger than grief.

Outside, the wind shifted.

Somewhere beyond the horizon, the sea waited, vast and familiar.

And in the heart of the camp, Paari's little diya burned on, as if the river itself had found them again.

The Sindhu River becomes the symbol of Sindhi endurance and dignity — a living lineage flowing through mother Paari and son Bajo.

Chapter 10

The Market Place of Hope

Morning in Valivade came without bells, without the smell of cardamom tea or temple bells.

The sun rose pale and tired over the rows of wooden barracks, and dust hung in the air like unspoken sorrow.

But for Paari, every dawn was a beginning.

She had lived through famine and flood, through the day the world had turned upside down.

She had watched cities burn — but she had also seen them rebuilt.

When she looked at the camp, she did not see ruins.

She saw a place waiting to remember itself.

One morning, while men queued for grain rations and women fetched water from tin drums, Paari stood by a patch of open ground.

"This is where we'll begin," she said.

Bajo frowned.

"Begin what, Amma?" "A market," she replied simply.

"Every Sindhi heart needs a bazaar." The others laughed at first.

What could they sell?

They had nothing but hunger and hand-me-downs.

But Paari's conviction was contagious.

She spoke like someone who'd already seen the finished picture.

Within days, the empty stretch began to change.

Someone spread an old dupatta on the ground to display bangles.

Another laid out hand-woven mats.

Some boys gathered wood scraps and built small tables.

It wasn't much, but it felt alive.

And for the first time since Sindh, the camp echoed with the sound of trade again — haggling, laughter, the rhythm of life returning.

When the camp officer came by, he asked Paari where she'd learned to organize people so quickly.

She smiled.

"From the river," she said.

"It doesn't ask permission to flow.

It just finds its way." Paari taught the women to barter fairly, to weave and embroider, to roll the kind of phulkas that stayed soft for days.

Soon, the small marketplace began to attract people from neighboring camps — buying, selling, exchanging stories.

Bajo, Anand, Bansi, Lolu got up early in the morning and together, they walked to Shivaji Putala Market in Kolhapur.

At night, Paari would look around the flickering lights of their new bazaar — lanterns swaying gently in the warm breeze — and whisper to herself, "The river flows again." But not everyone was kind.

One day, a local trader from the nearby town came into the camp.

Seeing their makeshift stalls, he mocked them.

"You refugees think you can compete with the real merchants?" he sneered.

Paari rose slowly from where she sat, her dupatta drawn over her silver hair.

Her gaze was steady, her voice quiet but fierce.

"We are Sindhis," she said.

"We have traded with the world.

We do not compete — we create." The man shifted uneasily, muttered something under his breath, and left.

By the next day, he was back — this time to buy her khataainn {pickles} and papads to sell in his own shop.

Over the weeks, Valivade changed.

Where once there had been despair, there was now enterprise — small, determined, dignified.

Paari became the camp's quiet leader, her presence like the flame of her old diya, steady through every gust of hardship.

Bajo began to see that what she had said on the road from Sindh was true: "You can lose everything outside you, but you must not lose the goodness inside you." Now he understood what that meant.

Goodness was not meekness.

It was strength with grace.

It was the power to build without bitterness, to trade without greed, to share without pride.

That night, Paari sat by her diya again, the brass glinting softly in the lamplight.

She looked at her family — tired, laughing, alive.

The air smelled of fried potatoes and cardamom.

Somewhere, a child was humming the tune of an old Sindhi song.

Paari smiled.

The sea was far away, but the spirit of the Sindhu was right here — flowing through every heart that refused to give up.

The marketplace was small, but it was theirs.

Their new world had begun.

"When you have nothing," Paari would later tell her grandchildren, "make something — even if it's just a little market of hope."

Chapter 11

Valiwade Refugees' Camp

It held thousands of souls torn from their homeland, stitched together by grief and survival.

The mornings were worst.

Before the sun dared open its eyes, the shrill scream of the train ripped through the darkness, and suddenly the whole camp erupted—men and women rushing with bundles on their backs, on their heads, in arms tired of carrying too much for too long.

They ran as if chased by fate itself.

It was chaos.

It was routine.

It was life—such as it was.

People had roofs now, if one could call them that.

Four walls and a blanket.

A place where their bodies lay down at night, but their memories never did.

The greatest struggle wasn't the pain of the past.

It was the daily battle for the basic things: flour, milk, a little dignity.

Milk powder—once promised twice a week—had vanished like a ghost.

Blankets and lamps came only once, as if stamped for display, not survival.

The government's enthusiasm burned bright for a

moment and then went dark, like a matchstick that dies as soon as it is lit.

Nobody dared ask what had happened.

Nobody wanted to believe the answer.

The camp slept uneasily in the hours before dawn, the silence broken only by the hum of insects—tiny creatures keeping vigil while the humans dreamed of what they had lost.

It was fifteen minutes to four when Bajo's breathing changed.

His snoring faded, replaced by restless turning.

A voice soon rose outside his barrack.

"Bajo... eh, Bajo... get up.

It's four." Another joined in.

"Come on, Bajo—we have to leave." Bajo stepped outside to find Bansi, Radho, Lolu, Jumdo, and young Arjun—his morning companions—waiting in the cold.

They were not just walking companions.

They were lifelines.

Brothers bound not by blood, but loss.

Seven miles.

Every morning.

Seven miles to Kolhapur, to Bamanpuri bazaar, to scrape together enough rupees to keep their families breathing.

That morning, something felt heavier in the air—like a storm waiting to break.

"The shine of the bride lasted nine days," Bansi muttered bitterly, shaking in the cold.

"What do you mean?" Bajo asked.

"That the government's affection was only a show," Bansi sighed.

"A wedding with no marriage." Milk powder was the sore wound.

Women had whispered its disappearance for days.

Bajo had ignored it—thinking it was everyday complaint.

But now the men's voices trembled with the same frustration.

"No milk powder," Bansi mocked the officials.

"This week... next... who knows," muttered Lolu.

"No order yet," Jumdo added.

"All lies.

All tricks.

All cruelty," Bansi concluded.

Bajo listened in silence—something breaking inside him.

He tried to defend the system out of habit, or perhaps fear.

"The government has lakhs to care for... we must understand." "We have been only understanding, Bajo," Lolu murmured, and the weight in his voice crushed any argument.

Later that evening, in a Kolhapur medical store, Bajo saw it.

There, behind shiny glass—like trophies—lay tins of milk powder.

The same tins the camp had been denied for weeks.

The same tins mothers needed to feed their babies.

"You get free milk powder, don't you?" the shopkeeper asked casually, as though discussing the weather.

"Hmmm..." "Sell me your extra tins.

Half price." Half price!

Bajo felt dizzy—as if the room were spinning.

The milk that starving children cried for... sold behind glass...like a luxury.

His hands trembled.

His throat tightened.

He took his change and walked out into a world that suddenly looked darker.

The next morning, he didn't walk to Kolhapur.

His legs carried him somewhere else—towards justice, or at least the hope of it.

One by one, men joined him.

By noon, over 150 refugees stood with him, hearts beating like drums, unified by anger and desperation.

The Collector—Nanjappa—arrived with officers, strutting through the camp as if they walked among beggars, not human beings.

The camp had been cleaned hurriedly for his visit, as if dirt was the biggest shame.

As refugees gathered around, questions burst forth like a dam breaking.

"How does the milk disappear?" "Where does our ration go?" "Is stealing from the hungry your service?" Each question was a wound reopened.

Collector Nanjappa snapped.

"You rascals... bloody refugees... you deserve to starve!" The words struck the crowd like a blade.

Mothers clutched their children closer.

Men felt tears burn behind their eyes—tears of humiliation more painful than hunger.

A young man lunged—not out of rage, but out of the unbearable weight of being dehumanized.

The District Officer struck him viciously.

The air cracked.

Fury erupted.

A stone flew.

Then another.

Pain.

Panic.

Screams.

The Collector shouted, "Inspector—fire in the air!"

But the inspector didn't fire in the air.

The bullet tore through the crowd.

A sickening thud.

The sound no one ever forgets.

Lachhu fell.

Fourteen-year-old Lachhu.

The boy who walked with them every dawn.

Who joked.

Who dreamed.

Who had lost everything once already—and now lost even his right to breathe.

Blood pooled beneath him, soaking into the earth as if the ground itself mourned him.

Someone screamed his name.

Someone else covered their face.

Bansi fell to his knees.

Another shot.

Namomal cried out, clutching his bleeding leg.

The collector froze, horror etching itself across his face.

He had asked for fear, not death.

But now death lay at his feet.

And the Commandant—helpless, powerless, ashamed—felt his soul collapse.

This tragedy needed only gentleness, only honesty, only humanity.

Instead, it got a bullet.

And in that moment, every refugee knew their lives were cheaper than the tins of milk powder hidden behind glass.

Chapter 12

The Shadow of Loss

The stillness that descended over the Valivade refugee camp after Lachhu's killing was unlike anything the camp had ever known.

The boy was only fourteen—barely stepping into the threshold of youth—when he was shot by a police officer following the rash and merciless orders of Collector Ninjappa.

The news spread like wildfire, silencing laughter, bringing down the bustle of daily life to a dull hum of grief.

Major Misal, known to many in the camp as a steady hand in turbulent times, was helpless as the tragedy unfolded.

The bullet that took Lachhu's life also pierced the fragile hope of the displaced families, reminding them of the weight of their statelessness and the indifference of power.

Bajo, with his quiet strength, took it upon himself to visit Lachhu's shattered family.

His parents, eyes hollow with shock and disbelief, sat like stone figures outside their modest house in the barrack.

The mother's hands trembled continuously, a motion she seemed unaware of.

The father sat rigid, as if moving might shatter what little dignity he clung to.

Bajo knelt before them, broken by the same injustice.

He held their hands in silence, offering no empty words, only the warmth of solidarity.

The camp, too, began to gather, in a shared sense of loss that needed no language.

It was Bajo who first raised the idea of helping Kanhaiya, the younger brother.

Twelve years old, with the same mischievous eyes Lachhu had, but now dulled by the shadow of death. "We cannot let one more child be lost," Bajo whispered to Major Misal later that night, his voice thick with unshed tears. "If he can go to school… maybe there's still a future for him." Major Misal, hardened by his years of service yet softened by the suffering he witnessed daily, agreed without hesitation.

The very next morning, he arranged for Kanhaiya to attend the modest school set up within the camp—an institution built with threadbare resources but fierce determination.

Major Misal himself accompanied Bajo to Lachhu's family to convey this decision, staying with them longer than duty required, listening, grieving, assuring.

And so, amid the sorrow, the camp moved forward.

The people of Valivade—refugees from a land that no longer existed for them—leaned on each other in their darkest hour.

They brought food to Lachhu's family, kept them company through sleepless nights, and ensured that the boy's memory would not be swallowed by time or fear.

Kanhaiya, carrying his brother's name in his heart, walked to school each morning.

His books were second-hand, his clothes worn, but his eyes began, slowly, to regain a glimmer of hope.

That is how Valivade endured.

Resilient.

Supportive.

A community woven together by loss, but held firm by compassion.

Chapter 13

Embers Beneath the Ashes

The days that followed Lachhu's death settled over the Valivade camp like a heavy fog.

The grief was no longer sharp—it dulled into something quieter but more dangerous, something that burned deep in the bones of the people.

Yet life, in its stubborn way, insisted on moving forward.

Major Misal's visits to Lachhu's parents became more frequent.

At first, he was met with silence—resentful, brittle silence that cut deeper than words.

He understood it.

In some ways, he shared it.

The image of Lachhu's lifeless body haunted his nights.

For the first time in years, the Major—a man trained to obey, to survive, to remain detached—found himself questioning everything.

Bajo, too, was restless.

A man of the people, he could not look away.

Together, Bajo and the Major took small steps to stitch the boy's family back into the fragile social fabric of the camp.

They arranged for Kanhaiya's schooling, made sure food reached the family, and even saw to it that some of the older boys in the camp took the younger child under their wing.

But there was an unease growing—something deeper than grief.

The real thorn was Collector Ninjappa.

Word spread—quietly at first—that Ninjappa had ordered the killing without provocation, a show of power more than law.

His arrogance grew in the days after the shooting.

He rode into the camp with mounted police as if it were occupied territory, issuing orders with the careless cruelty of a man who viewed the refugees not as people but as a nuisance to be contained.

Major Misal, once deferential, now found himself caught between duty and conscience.

He began pushing back—discreetly at first.

He blocked some of Ninjappa's more excessive demands.

He refused to let the police harass the school children.

He made sure that camp rations, already meager, were not siphoned off for the collector's pet projects.

It was a dangerous line to walk.

One evening, as the sun bled into the horizon, Ninjappa summoned Major Misal to his bungalow on the hill overlooking the camp.

The collector's voice was sharp, his words laced with veiled threats.

"You're getting too sentimental, Major," Ninjappa said, swirling a glass of whisky as he stared down at the distant refugee camp.

"These people—vermin, really—they don't need sympathy.

They need control.

And if you're not prepared to provide it, I can find someone who will." Misal said nothing at first.

His hands, resting calmly at his sides, were clenched tight enough that his knuckles turned white.

Finally, he spoke: "With respect, sir, control isn't what keeps the camp from falling apart.

It's dignity.

Take that away, and you'll have something on your hands you won't be able to control." For a long moment, the two men locked eyes.

Ninjappa smirked, as if amused by a child's defiance, but said no more.

The message was clear.

That night, as Misal returned to the camp, he found Bajo waiting near the schoolhouse where Kanhaiya and the other children were still awake, giggling over their slates in the dim lamplight.

The sight made something inside the Major ache.

"We need to be careful," Misal said softly.

Bajo nodded.

"We also need to be brave." The seeds of quiet resistance had been planted.

The Valivade camp—battered but not broken—was beginning to find its voice.

The fragile calm of Valivade shattered further in the weeks that followed.

Collector Ninjappa, humiliated by Major Misal's quiet defiance, tightened his grip on the camp with a ruthless hand.

"We may be refugees," Bajo told a small circle one night, "but we are not animals.

We left behind homes, lands, even names—but not our right to dignity." Major Misal, sitting beside him in the flickering light of a kerosene lamp, said little.

His uniform still weighed on him—an iron reminder of the chain of command.

But his eyes betrayed him.

They had softened.

And they had hardened.

Kanhaiya sat nearby, pouring over his slate, the ghost of Lachhu forever in his shadow.

His presence—this small boy still clutching to hope—galvanized the men and women of Valivade in a way speeches never could.

Slowly, quietly, the camp began to organize.

Families shared food across lines of caste and language—once unthinkable.

And through it all, Major Misal walked a tightrope between rebellion and ruin.

That evening, as Bajo and Misal stood together under the weight of the gathering dusk, the Major finally spoke what had been brewing in his heart: "Ninjappa will not stop," he said quietly.

"And I cannot protect you forever."

Bajo's reply was steady.

"We understand, Major.

But stand with us.

That's all we ask." Major Misal nodded.

In the distance, the camp was alight with quiet voices, children's laughter returning in fragile bursts, and for the first time in months, the sound of someone singing softly under their breath.

The storm was far from over.

But the people of Valivade—resilient, supportive, defiant—were ready.

Chapter 14

Standing Tall

A child had died.
Not from violence this time, but from preventable illness.

And the camp could bear no more.

It was Bajo who gave the call, but the cry had already formed in every heart: "Enough." By dawn the next day, the people of Valivade gathered—thousands of them.

Men, women, children.

The young girls with defiant eyes, mothers carrying infants on their hips.

They came not with weapons, but with their voices, their bodies, their sheer will.

They marched from the heart of the camp to the district collector's office, barefoot under the blistering sun, carrying placards painted on old dupatta and torn flour sacks: "We Are Human." "We Demand Dignity." "Our Children Deserve Life." Major Misal stood at the head of the march.

He no longer pretended neutrality.

In his crisp but worn uniform, he marched beside Bajo, his every step a quiet act of rebellion.

He knew the risks.

Court martial.

Imprisonment.

Worse.

But he had made his choice.

The procession grew as they moved.

Farmers from nearby villages, tradesmen, even some sympathetic local clerks joined in hushed solidarity.

The air trembled with something raw, something unstoppable.

Collector Ninjappa, red-faced and livid, stood waiting with the police at the gates of his sprawling colonial bungalow.

He ordered his men to block the road.

He barked for arrests.

But the police hesitated.

They had seen the faces of the protestors: women carrying photographs of lost sons, children too thin from months of hunger, fathers with tears in their eyes but their spines unbent.

Some of the police themselves had families not so different.

They lowered their batons.

Ninjappa screamed.

Threatened.

Demanded.

But no one moved.

It was then that Major Misal stepped forward.

His voice, when it came, was soft but carried through the hushed crowd: "Sir, the people you see here are not enemies of the state.

They are the remnants of war, the survivors of exile.

We can no longer govern them through fear.

This ends today." For a long breathless moment, the world stood still.

Then, without warning, a telegram boy arrived on a rusted bicycle.

He dismounted, wiping the sweat from his brow, and handed Ninjappa a single sheet.

The collector's hands trembled as he read.

The order was brief: "Collector Ninjappa is hereby relieved of his duties and transferred out of Kolhapur District, effective immediately." The silence that followed was electric.

Ninjappa crumpled the paper, his face drained of color, and without a word, retreated inside.

The doors of the bungalow slammed shut behind him.

A murmur rose from the crowd.

Then a cry.

Then a roar.

Valivade had stood its ground.

In the days that followed, the mood in the camp transformed.

Bajo, with quiet determination, helped the camp move on.

Major Misal remained at his post but was no longer just an officer—he was one of them now, trusted, respected.

Kanhaiya returned to school.

His slate was still worn, his books still second-hand, but he walked taller.

His parents, though still hollowed by the loss of Lachhu, smiled for the first time in months.

The Valivade camp—scarred, battered, yet unbroken—moved forward.

Resilient.

Supportive.

Defiant.

And so history would remember them: not as silent victims, but as people who stood tall when it mattered most.

Chapter 15

The Bridge-Builder

The monsoon had arrived in Valivade.
Rain drummed on the roofs made of Mangalore tiles, turning the dust to red mud and the narrow lanes into rivers.

Children splashed through puddles, chasing paper boats that sank too soon.

For Bajo, the sound of water always carried stories — the echo of the Sindhu, the whisper of the sea, the call of movement.

But this time, the current inside him flowed toward the future.

After the marketplace took root, men would rise before dawn, sweep the mud from their stall, and light the small brass diya.

Bajo watched them every morning while leaving for the Kolhapur market.

"You must tend to light before you tend to trade," Bajo said.

"Business is not about profit — it is about purpose." His words stayed with him.

He realized that service itself could be a kind of commerce — the giving and taking of hope.

One afternoon, when the rain paused, a man from the nearby school came to the camp.

He needed someone to help unload supplies — books, slates, chalk.

While stacking crates, Bajo's cousin brother Nanu saw the books spill open — lines of neat writing, maps of distant lands, diagrams of ships and stars.

His heart beat faster.

The world seemed suddenly wide again.

The man noticed his curiosity.

"You read Sindhi?"

"Very well," Nanu said.

"My grandmother taught me the letters." "Then come tomorrow," the man replied.

"We need someone to teach the younger children." Nanu hesitated.

He was no teacher — just a refugee boy.

But Paari, hearing of it, smiled.

"Go, Nanu, " she said.

"Our ancestors traded goods; you will trade knowledge.

That, too, feeds people." The next week, Nanu began gathering children in the shade of a banyan tree.

They sat on the earth with bits of charcoal for pencils, writing alphabets in the dust.

He taught them the stories Paari had told him — of the river, of Meluhha, of how Sindhis once sailed to lands where the stars looked different but kindness was the same.

Word spread.

Soon even local village children joined them.

At first, some elders frowned — refugees and townsfolk learning together?

But Paari told them gently "When water meets water, do we ask which drop belongs to which cloud?" The phrase became an aphorism in the camp.

Nanu's open-air school grew into a school in a barrack.

One evening, a storm tore through Valivade.

The rain lashed, winds howled, and the roof of the new classroom collapsed.

Everyone ran for shelter.

Nanu stood in the storm, soaked, staring at the wreckage.

Paari came beside him, her dupatta whipping in the wind.

"Let it fall," she said softly.

"Now build it stronger." The next morning, the entire camp gathered to rebuild.

Men hammered, women brought food, children sang.

By nightfall, the classroom stood again — sturdier, brighter, a symbol of what they could do together.

Nanu realized that their real trade was not goods or grain — it was resilience.

She had bartered despair for dignity, and passed the skill to him.

Months later, officials visiting the camp stopped to see the small school.

They promised more books, more aid.

As they left, one of them asked Paari how such order existed in a place born of exile.

She smiled, eyes gleaming in the lamplight.

"Because we do not wait for bridges to be built for us," she said.

"We build them — one hand, one heart, one plank at a time." That night, Bajo shared his mother's words with Nanu.

He wrote those words on the classroom wall.

The children copied them carefully, each letter a promise.

Outside, the monsoon eased.

The stars returned.

And somewhere beyond the rain-washed sky, the Sindhu flowed on — carrying their story forward, from river to sea, from Paari to Bajo, from the past into the shining unknown.

"To trade is to connect," Paari would say.

"And the best trade of all is kindness.

Chapter 16

Seven Miles to Kolhapur

The February mornings in Valivade were still cold enough to bite.

The fog clung to the fields, and the dew settled on the roofs of the barracks like a thin blessing.

Bajo woke before dawn.

He moved quietly so as not to wake the children.

His wife, Bhagyavanti, handed him a small parcel of phulkas and a large cup of tea.

Paari, already awake, sat by the flickering diya.

"Go early, come safe," she said.

"And remember — we do not just carry goods, we carry our name." Bajo smiled and stepped into the mist.

Seven miles of red mud and silence lay between Valivade and Kolhapur.

The men walked in a small group — Anand, Bansi, Lolu, and a few others from the camp — their breath rising like smoke in the cool air.

Sometimes they sang old Sindhi folk tunes, sometimes they walked in quiet determination, the rhythm of their footsteps steady as faith.

They carried baskets of potatoes, onions, and garlic, bought with some money that was saved and sold for small margins in the bustling Bamanpuri and Shivaji Markets of Kolhapur.

The journey was long.

The profit, modest.

But it was theirs.

Each morning, as the city's noise grew louder — the clang of the bullock cart bells, the cry of vendors, the scent of fried snacks in the air, Bajo felt something stir inside him.

He was not just a refugee anymore.

He was a trader — like those ancient ancestors who once sailed from Sindhu to Mesopotamia.

Bajo smiled and remembered Sindbad, the Sailor.

He wondered, " Sindbad, the Sailor!

Wasn't Sindbad a Sindhi!" The markets were alive with color and chaos — piles of red onions glistening in the sun, women bargaining in Marathi, bullock carts creaking under sacks of grain.

At first, the city merchants mocked them — "Refugees trying to sell our vegetables?" But Paari's lessons had prepared Bajo better than any classroom could.

He smiled, weighed the produce fairly, spoke gently, and returned the change without fuss.

Soon, the customers began to seek him out.

"That Sindhi boy gives, whatever we buy, in full measure," they'd say, And his garlic is clean, his onions don't rot." By the third month, the group's earnings began to grow.

Bajo saved a few rupees every day — hidden carefully in a small brass box under mother Paari's cot.

As dusk fell, they walked back — feet blistered, shoulders aching, but spirits high.

Sometimes they joked about their aching legs.

Sometimes they walked in silence, the stars coming out one by one above the darkening fields.

When they reached Valivade, the camp would already be lit with lamps.

The smell of daal and spice filled the air.

The women would be waiting — Paari among them, sitting tall, her eyes bright with quiet pride.

Bajo would hand her a small bag of jaggery or tea leaves.

"For you, Amma." She would touch his head gently.

"Our trade continues," she'd say.

Bhagyavanti would bring him a glass of water.

Anand, the younger brother, would also touch his mother's feet, she would bless him.

In time, Bajo and his brother Anand pooled their savings together and bought a small shop and painted it bright blue.

Across the front, they wrote in bold Sindhi and Marathi letters: " Bajomal Parchomal & Brothers...

Wholesale Merchants." Soon their shop became a familiar sight in Kolhapur.

Local shopkeepers began to respect them.

One even offered to partner with them, but Paari advised caution.

"Never sell your name," she said.

"It's worth more than your goods." Months later, when Bajo returned home after selling a full cartload, Paari asked how much he'd earned.

Bajo placed the money before her, gleaming in the lamplight.

She didn't count them.

Instead, she picked one coin up, pressed it into his palm, and said: "This is not just money.

This is memory.

The same hands that once built ports and traded across seas have built again — with sweat instead of sails."

Bajo felt his throat tighten.

He looked at the dark marks on his palms — the proof of work, of worth.

That night, as rain pattered softly on the roofs, Paari lit the diya again.

Its flame flickered, steady and golden — like the dawn that waited for them every morning, seven miles away.

Paari said, The Sindhu flows within us when it cannot find the sea, it creates one

Chapter 17

Poet of the Two Worlds

If you stroll through Valivade, Kolhapur, today, it's hard to imagine that this peaceful suburb was once home to thousands of displaced families from Sindh, each clutching memories, hope, and a few brass utensils wrapped in cloth.

Among them, sometime after the Partition dust had barely settled, a baby boy was born—Shashi Gajwani—in a refugee camp that smelled of both despair and determination. 'The Poet' became his unofficial title before he even got his first ration card.

But little did anyone know that this baby boy, who grew up playing marbles in the camp lanes, would one day make Marathi film stars hum his poetry and college students quote his songs in their love letters, '' Naata tujha ni maajha, julala kasa te kalalach naahin, majhyaa Priye..'' Shashi's parents, Bajomal and Bhagyavanti, grandparents Paari and Parchomal, great grandparents Bakhat and Jadalmal, were practical people.

After surviving Partition, they had little patience for sentimentality—unless it came in rhyme.

They sold onions and potatoes by day and told stories of Sindh by night.

"We left behind our land, but not our language," Paari would say, stirring dal as she recited Sindhi couplets with dramatic flair.

Shashi, however, was already being seduced by the sound of another tongue—the lilting music of Marathi that filled Kolhapur's lanes.

He found it fascinating that the same word could sound so much more musical when spoken by his Marathi friends.

"Aai ga!" had a rhythm that matched so fascinatingly with the Sindhi "Amma!" At school, his notebooks had both Sindhi proverbs and Marathi metaphors, jostling for space.

When asked which language he preferred, he'd grin and say, "Whichever one rhymes better today."

By sixteen, while other boys were still saving for bicycles, Shashi had become a published poet in Maharashtra's respected newspapers and magazines- Pudhari , Maratha, Swarajya.

He started as a contributor but was soon invited to join the legendary newspaper Pudhari's editorial desk.

The editors called him "the boy who edits commas like a surgeon." He, in turn, called them "My adorable colleagues who drink too much chai and debate adjectives." Years later, when Shashi had transitioned from a newspaper poet to a lyricist and screenwriter, his wife Shraddha entered the story—quite literally carrying it in her hands.

His wife Shraddha was his trusted listener, a title that sounds less exciting until you imagine her driving across Mumbai's streets with handwritten script of Aakhreen Train – The Last Train, tucked under her arm like a state secret.

The two shared a relationship built on words, wit, and a mutual inability to meet a deadline.

Once, while delivering a draft, Shraddha asked him: "Shashiji, you've written the heroine's death scene three different ways.

Which one do I give them?"
He replied,
"Depends.
Are they paying for drama or realism this week?" Their back-and-forth became legendary among friends—a poet and his co-author, laughing their way through rewrites and rewinds.

Aakhreen Train – The Last Train, based on the legendary Thakur Chawla's Sindhi story, was a film close to Shashi's heart.

It traced the emotional journey of Partition survivors— something they knew not from history books, but from the stories they heard and experienced from their childhood.

Yet, amidst the creative pressure, their writing sessions were anything but somber.

He'd often break into impromptu songs mid-sentence, humming half-written verses before scribbling them down on the nearest newspaper margin.

Shraddha, ever the organized one, would give him that extra paper.

"Your genius," she said once, "is allergic to stationery." One day, when the dialogue for a key scene refused to come, Shraddha looked up from her notes and said, "Maybe the characters don't want to speak today." Shashi Gajwani replied, "Then make them sing." She did— and that became the haunting song, Chhothee dil chaahe.. the vibrant AakhreenTrain -The Last Train song picturised on the talented Simran Ahuja and Hrishika Gangwani.

Kolhapur had raised warriors and saints—but in Shashi, it found a poet with laughter in his pocket and language in his soul.

If there's one thing Shashi Gajwani loved as much as words, it was timing—both in verse and in jokes.

His friends said he could write a tragic song about heartbreak and, two minutes later, make the recording studio burst into laughter.

During the recording of Naata Tujha ni Maajha, for his Marathi film, Raakhandaar, the studio's power failed.

While the composer Vishwanath More panicked, Shashi said, "Don't worry, Vishwanath, darkness improves emotion.

Even heartbreak sounds better when you can't see the bill." He wrote the last stanza by matchlight—and it went on to light up millions of hearts.

He wrote this famous song from Mulgi Zhaali Ho while waiting for lunch.

Marnaalaa saang tu thaamb zaraa...

"The line came to me because I was hungry," he admitted.

"And hunger is the best lyricist." Shraddha remained his partner-in-creativity.

She chased him for deadlines and deciphered his poetic handwriting that looked like monsoon on paper.

"Shashi!

The producer's waiting!" she'd yell.

"I'm waiting too," he'd reply.

"For divine inspiration—or the black tea?" Shraddha would ask. " Whichever comes first." Shashi would say with a smile.

When his Hindi song Jab Dil Machal Jaataa Hai from Doosra Ghar went viral decades later, he asked, "Viral?

Should I take antibiotics?" He laughed when someone credited Shashi Kapoor instead of him: "Why waste good fame?" Shashi's humour turned every studio session into theatre.

When a chorus went missing for Gaav Ek Numberi, he asked the assistant directors to do the chorus: "They've been shouting all day anyway." The result?

Authentic village energy!

He called songs "Ecstasy in rhyme." For him, a song was never a filler—it was soul.

If you visit Shashi Gajwani's Kolhapur home, two things will always be on: his Bluetooth speaker and his pen.

One plays Hemant Kumar; the other outwrites time.

Morning tea was Hemant's melody; " Yeh raat , yeh chandni, phir kahaan, Sunn ja dil ki daastaan." Evening meant Kishore Kumar's magic.

Dil aaj shayar hai, Gham aaj naghma hai, Shab yeh ghazal hai, Sanam...': Shashi sang along—loudly, proudly, and occasionally off-key.

"Why should Kishore have all the fun?" he'd grin.

His desk looked like a cyclone of creativity.

"Poetry doesn't stop," he'd say.

"It just changes fonts." His Hindi anthology *Fisalte Lamhon Ko Chhoote Chhoote* was his love letter to time.

"It's a diary that accidentally rhymed," he explained.

Readers called it profound; he called it "Self-defense against seriousness." A five-minute chat could stretch to three hours—half philosophy, half playlist.

He'd say things like: "Earlier songs had emotions" Shraddha would quip, " ...now they have Wi-Fi." And then sip black chai like someone who'd just solved global harmony.

He adored Hemant Kumar for calmness and Kishore Kumar for courage.

"Between them," he said, "I stay sane." He is an affectionate critic of the film industry.

"The beat may change," he said, "but the heart shouldn't." Producers found his metaphors expensive.

"Poetry," Shraddha would tell them, "is like tea — you can't boil it for speed." Shashi joked that humour was his best weapon against melancholy.

"Life already writes enough tragedy.

I just add the rhymes." Every poet has a metaphor that never leaves him.

For Shashi Gajwani, it was the train.

It began with his family's escape from Sindh in 1947 and echoed through their film Aakhreen Train – The Last Train.

But his "last train" was never about endings — it was about continuity.

"The Partition took away our land," he said once, "but not our resolve." He described Valivade as "childhood on platform number one." When asked how he became a poet, he replied: "When you're born in a barrack, you learn that walls are optional." His songs carried Kolhapur's soil and Sindh's sand — two worlds meeting in melody.

Fame didn't dazzle him; he said it was just "a friendly co-passenger." His poetry collection Fisalte Lamhon Ko Chhoote Chhoote captured the music of memory.

"It's just my poems gossiping with each other," he said.

Even in his frequent stay in the US, he wrote daily.

"Life is a flight," he once wrote.

"Sometimes fast, sometimes delayed, but every layover has a new verse waiting." And so the poet keeps travelling — through his songs, his humour, and his words that refuse to stay still.

The train moves on, softly, eternally — like a Kishore Kumar song merging into the mystical night.

Shashi Gajwani loves his metaphors, pen in hand, a smile on his face, writing his way through mornings, melodies, and monsoons.

Every dawn begins with a hum — a bit of Hemant Kumar for grace, a burst of Kishore Kumar for mischief, and a fresh page daring him to begin again.

By noon, his desk is a happy battlefield, ink stains, black tea cups, paper slips, and laughter.

He still writes the way he lives— spontaneous, rhythmic, and rebelliously alive.

"Deadlines are like trains," he jokes, "miss one, and another will whistle soon — just keep your energy and passion flowing." His anthology, Fisalte Lamhon Ko Chhoote Chhoote, keeps growing — like a vine of moments twining around time's old backyard.

Sometimes it sings of Valivade's red dust, sometimes of love that refuses to fade, and sometimes of life itself — that glorious, unpredictable poem.

Shashi doesn't chase nostalgia; he befriends it.

He argues with memory, teases sorrow, and lets the past go with a wink and a couplet.

For him, every emotion deserves a melody— and every silence, a smile.

Kolhapur remains his compass — its lanes echoing with verses, its sunsets humming his refrains.

He still strolls to his favourite café, humming old film tunes, scribbling lines on napkins that end up as verses in tomorrow's films.

Ask him about how he continues writing with so much feeling, and he'll laugh softly, eyes gleaming: "Life is so charming!

It's a wonder.

And I am wonder struck!" The poet of two worlds still walks both — one foot in memory, one in mischief.

Every word he writes is a bridge, every smile, a stanza, every heartbeat, a song that says — "The train still runs, the journey still sings, and I — I am still on board." Shashi is proud of his parents and the way they worked hard to live a life of dignity and joy.

He says with a smile, "I was born in a refugee camp — not exactly a palace, but I found poetry in the brick walls.

I heard songs in the Kolhapur hills.

The world gave me languages; I gave them songs.

I've never believed in borders — not of land, not of art, not even of age.

If a word can travel from Sindh to Kolhapur, from a refugee camp to a cinema screen — then maybe we are all poets, just waiting for the right rhythm to find us.

I still hum when it rains, still write when it's sunny, and still believe that laughter is the most honest lyric.

My train hasn't stopped yet — it just takes longer halts for black tea now.

When you love life, poetry follows....

Chapter 18

The letter that found its way

Shashi had heard of the Polish cemetery in Kolhapur. Every year, a large group of Polish people visited Kolhapur, coming all the way from Poland, the US and Europe, to pay respect to their dear departed souls who died during their settlement in the Valivade refugee Camp during the Second World War.

Shashi decided to find out more about it and heard a story that was nothing less than a miracle.

Bombay, 1943.

Even the air felt restless.

The Second World War had scattered people like dry leaves before a storm, blowing families into different continents with no promise of reunion.

Ships crossed seas under blackout rules, soldiers healed in distant hospitals, mothers waited for the sons, and children watched skies that carried both hope and dread.

Yet in this fractured world, sometimes—just sometimes—the universe found a way to mend what war had torn apart.

Inside the Polish Red Cross headquarters in Bombay, the volunteers moved between tables stacked with relief parcels, name registers, and the lists of the missing.

One humid afternoon, a Red Cross officer rang a small brass bell and addressed a roomful of Indian and Polish schoolchildren gathered around him.

They sat cross-legged on the floor, their eyes bright with curiosity.

"Children," he began, "there are Polish soldiers wounded in hospitals all over the world.

Many have lost contact with their families.

They need hope.

They need to know that someone remembers them." He paused, searching the young faces.

"Will you write to them?" A murmur rippled through the room—excitement, shyness, uncertainty.

The children did not know it yet, but someone in that room would change a life, far away and unseen.

Hundreds of miles away, in the quiet refuge of the Valivade Camp in Kolhapur, India, the mornings began with dust and sunlight.

The camp was home to thousands of Polish refugees—women, children, the elderly—souls uprooted by war and replanted in unfamiliar soil.

Every morning at nine, the camp sergeant marched in with his satchel stuffed with letters.

The children awaited him like sparrows waiting for crumbs of the outside world.

He would call out in his sonorous voice, softened by affection: "Would you like to write a letter to an unknown soldier today?" The little ones giggled.

The older children nodded solemnly.

But two sisters—Mita and Alina Turowicz—felt the question resonate with unusual depth.

Alina gripped her younger sister's arm.

"Mita, should we?" Mita, thoughtful beyond her years, said, "Someone out there is lonely.

We can't let loneliness win." And so they wrote.

At the same time, in the glittering heat of Heliopolis,

Egypt, young Maria Kurzawski, a cadet in the Airman School, sat on her narrow bed in the dormitory.

Letters were her lifeline.

Each week, she received news from her mother and sister in India—two anchors in a world that felt as unstable as shifting sand.

One evening, her instructor approached.

"Maria, the Red Cross has asked cadets to volunteer as pen pals for Polish children in camps.

Would you like to write to a couple of girls?" Maria's smile was immediate.

"I would love to." She was given two names.

Two girls in need of a friend.

One was in Africa.

The other in India.

Mita Turowicz, Valivade Camp.

The connection began with small, careful letters—descriptions of daily life, questions about each other's world.

Neither girl knew that ink and goodwill were weaving something far greater than simple friendship.

By December, the Valivade camp was preparing for a war-time Christmas.

The children made decorations from scraps—tinsel from tin foil, stars from ration paper, ornaments from pressed wildflowers.

Hope, in those days, was stitched from whatever the world had left behind.

In their small barrack room, Mita and Alina sat cross-legged on the floor, crafting a Christmas card for their faraway friend.

The paper was uneven.

The colors, faded.

The drawing, a tiny Bethlehem star.
But the message glowed with pure-hearted warmth.
"May light find you wherever you are.
With love— Mita & Alina." They placed it in an envelope, wrote "Cadet Maria Kurzawski, Heliopolis," and handed it to the camp post office.

Neither girl could imagine that the letter had already chosen a different destiny.

Somewhere along the labyrinth of wartime postal routes—routes broken by censored mail, rerouted ships, bombed rail lines, and overworked clerks—the letter took a strange turn.

It did not sail to Egypt.

It did not walk through the doors of Maria's school.

Instead, it traveled north, as if tugged by invisible strings— through ports, military channels, rerouted postal bags—until it landed in the fog-shrouded aisles of a military hospital in Scotland.

There lay Sergeant Jan Kurzawski, a Polish soldier wounded in battle.

A man who had not heard his daughters' voices since the early days of the war.

A man who whispered their names into his pillow before falling asleep.

"Maria… Alina…

Where are you now?" Nurses heard the yearning in his murmurs.

They exchanged glances of quiet sorrow.

One winter morning, a nurse approached with an envelope.

"Sergeant Kurzawski, this came for you.

We cannot explain how." He frowned.

"I'm not expecting any mail." But when he opened the card and saw the names signed at the bottom, the world seemed to tilt.

Mita.

And Alina.

For a moment, he could not breathe.

His daughter's name—Alina—written in a child's hand.

Destiny had not merely knocked.

It had thrown open the door.

The Christmas card was meant for Maria.

But it reached her father first.

A mistake?

Or something deeper?

Jan pressed the letter to his forehead, closing his eyes as tears—long held back by war—escaped into his hands.

"My daughters... They live.

They live..." The nurse placed a gentle hand on his shoulder.

"Then this letter was meant for you." Word spread quickly through the Red Cross network.

Within weeks, threads of communication reconnected the Kurzawski family across three continents—Scotland, India, Egypt.

Maria and Alina learned the impossible: their father was alive.

Jan learned that his daughters were safe.

And Mita—the gentle girl who acted out of nothing more than kindness—had unknowingly become the messenger chosen by fate.

In the years that followed, whenever the story was retold, people asked: "How could a letter addressed to

Egypt find its way to a specific soldier in Scotland?

How could it arrive at the exact moment he prayed for a sign?" Some called it coincidence.

Others called it luck.

But those who had lived through the war—who had seen entire worlds fall apart—knew better.

They understood that sometimes, in the darkest hours, the universe rearranges itself just enough to let one beam of light slip through.

This was one such light.

A handmade Christmas card.

Two sisters in a refugee camp.

A cadet across the sea.

A father on a hospital bed.

A path no map could chart.

A miracle!

Chapter 19

Polish Refugees in Valivade

The year was 1942.
Europe was torn apart by war, Poland lay in ruins—invaded, partitioned, and suffocating under the twin shadows of Nazi brutality and Soviet repression.

Families were ripped from their homes, deported to distant gulags, or left wandering the wastelands of war without country or kin.

Thousands of Polish citizens — many of them women and children — found themselves hurled into the icy wilderness of Siberia.

There, in Soviet labour camps, death came silently: through frostbite, starvation, or despair.

Children scavenged for roots beneath snow.

Mothers clung to the living while burying the dead.

Fathers, when present, were ghosts working themselves to the bone in forced labour.

From this abyss, a flicker of salvation emerged — not from the West, but from an unexpected corner of the East: India.

It was Kira Banasinska, the wife of the Polish Consul General in Mumbai, who first envisioned a refuge for these displaced souls.

With a heart fired by determination, she worked tirelessly with Indian officials, diplomats, and relief workers.

Slowly, carefully, an escape route was charted — crossing hostile terrain and wartime supply lines.

And in 1943, the first Polish refugees arrived in a quiet Maharashtrian village called Valivade, near Kolhapur.

The refugees arrived exhausted — gaunt, hollow-eyed, unsure.

The villagers of Valivade, guided by the humanitarian vision of the Bhosale royal family, met them not with suspicion, but with open hearts.

Inspired by the values of Chhatrapati Shivaji Maharaj, the Kolhapur rulers believed that dharma — true righteousness — meant standing for the vulnerable.

Valivade, once a sleepy hamlet, began to transform.

Schools, bakeries, carpentry sheds, and prayer halls were built.

For five years, from 1943 to 1948, this settlement became known as "Little Poland." But the real magic happened not in the buildings, but between people — in the dusty lanes, at market stalls, over shared meals, and on the playing fields.

Each morning, as the Polish camp woke up, Marathi vegetable vendors would arrive with bullock carts of fresh farm produce and set up their vegetable stalls with potatoes, onions, leafy green vegetables, carrots, green peas, tomatoes, capsicum, radish, cucumber, tamarind, across the fence of the camp.

They spoke no Polish.

The Polish women, still unfamiliar with Marathi, often pointed, gestured, mimed their way through every purchase.

A young Polish woman, Zofia, would smile shyly and point to a pile of tomatoes.

"Tomatoes?" she'd ask, fingers raised.

"Teen paise, haan?" An old vendor, Namdev, would reply, miming three fingers, his toothless smile as bright as the morning sun.

"Teen!

Yes!" Anna would echo, proud of her tiny victory over the language barrier.

Another woman, Teresa, drew little pictures of vegetables in a worn notebook to ask for cabbage, potatoes, or chillies.

The vendor's wife, Savitri, once laughed so hard she gifted her a free mango just for effort.

"Yevdha motha aamba!

Such a big mango!" she said, holding up the mango with both hands.

Helena couldn't understand the words, but the laughter needed no translation. The real bridges were built by the children.

One day, a ragged football rolled from the village side into the camp.

A boy named Vithal, all knees and elbows, chased after it and waved to the Polish children.

One girl, Anya, picked it up and kicked it back.

No words were needed.

The game began.

"Goal!" Stela would shout.

"Shabaash!" cheered Vithal..

They formed teams—blonde-haired Polish girls running barefoot beside Marathi boys, dusty and grinning.

What they shared wasn't language, but joy.

Marathi women taught the Polish refugees how to fry bhajjii, make bhakri, and roast poha over open fires.

In return, Polish women introduced them to warm

beet soup (barszcz) and dumplings (pierogi), shaped by hand and cooked over smoky stoves.

One afternoon, a Marathi boy bit into a pierogi and declared, "Kaay masst aahe!" The Polish cook beamed.

"Masst," she repeated.

"Good?"

He nodded enthusiastically.

"Ho, ho!" The kitchen became a place of laughter, taste, and shared discovery.

When Diwali came, the Polish children stared in wonder at the flickering diyas lining village homes.

Curious, they followed the light — and were welcomed with sweets and bangles.

"Try, try!" said Savitri, handing karanjis to a Polish girl named Marta.

Marysia took a bite and laughed.

"Mmm... dobre!" "Karanji!" Savitri laughed back.

That winter, for Christmas, the Polish families invited the villagers to a candlelit Mass.

They crafted stars from bamboo and paper, placed clay animals in a handmade Nativity scene — helped by local potters and curious children who whispered, "Dev?"

"Jesus," answered a Polish boy gently.

Two faiths stood side by side that night — not in conversion, but in communion.

Most refugees left after 1948, resettled in the West or returned to Poland.

But some hearts remained tethered to Valivade.

One unforgettable story is that of Wanda Nowicka, a Polish woman who fell in love with Vasant Kashikar, a Marathi man.

They married, raised five children, and Wanda became

"Malti," wearing saris and cooking upma alongside pierogi.

"We are still in touch with our Polish relatives," her children said years later.

"But Valivade will always be special for us." In 2014, the Polish cemetery in Kolhapur was restored — a quiet monument to those who found peace far from home.

The story of Valivade is not just a historical footnote — it is a luminous thread woven into the history of India and Poland's shared soul.

A story where strangers became family.

Where games replaced grief.

Where vegetables, songs, and broken phrases stitched together what war had torn apart.

Even today, long after the last Polish refugee had left, the whisper of that time lingers in Valivade's soil — in the rustle of leaves, the scent of pickled cucumbers, the echoes of "Shabaash!" and "Dzien dobry!" still carried on the wind.

Let it never be forgotten.

What was it like living in the Valivade Polish refugee camp?

Chapter 20

The Second World War

Polish refugees Changing places after places....from one place to another......these changes were the only constant in an otherwise uncertain life.

There was no energy left even to keep a count of the number of places changed.

When would this stop?

Was Valiwade Halt the last change?

Because before we moved in here, Valiwade was the camp inhabited by the Polish refugees.

But even these refugees had returned to their homeland Poland after five years.

Valiwade Halt.....

Before the Valivade camp was built, this was a vacant land loaned to the Polish government by Kolhapur Darbar.

The Maharaja was only three years old. 'Valiwade Halt railway was established in April 1944 for the Polish camp.

The Polish refugees were moved here.

The King of Kolhapur State Chhatrapati Rajaram Maharaj came here, rarely, just once in about six months.

Valiwade Halt was a secluded place with no sign of any human being anywhere near it.

No houses, no cottages, no shops.

Nothing.

There was no imprint of human existence in this area of silence.

There were only tree and plants all over the place.

And a lake full of blue water.

A flourishing green was the dominant colour in the atmosphere.

A lone gate was the only symbol of construction of the period.

The Valiwade village was nearby with a population of four hundred inhabitants.

Those were the days of the Second World War.

Major political upheavals had engulfed the entire world.

Fear had spread its ominous shadow over the world.

Thousands were killed and hundreds of planes were crashed every passing day.

Numerous ships and submarines were sunk.

Mankind was being dragged into extinction because of Hitler's ruthless ambition.

The value of human life was nothing more than an ant crushed under the sinister feet.

Men trapped in the jaws of death were trying to escape from it.

Innocent children, the frail, and the old...the young men and women... everyone... who doesn't love life?

Some were pulled away from their soil, so that they could live.

They had no choice but to leave their homeland, and live as refugees somewhere else.

The government had issued an ordinance that the refugees from Poland were to be sent to various places in India.

The Refugees' camps were to be constructed in some

selected places in Maharashtra and Valiwade Halt was one of the refugee-camps.

The year was 1943.

Permission for building of the camp in Valiwade was given on February 19, 1943.

The contract of erecting the camp was given to the Hindusthan company.

Hundreds of workers laboured on it.

The labour was also brought over from outside the State of Kolhapur.

Depending on the kind of work and the skill, the labour was paid three annas per day (one Indian rupee, in 1940's, was equal to sixteen annas = 64 paise).

The Valivade Camp was built specifically for the Polish refugees by the Public Works Department of the Government of India on behalf of the Polish government in London, who paid approximately Rs. 32 lacs for it, along with its equipment.

As the Poles did not have qualified staff in India at the time, the supervision of its construction by the Hindusthan Construction Co. was carried out by Lt.

Col. J. D. Condie, himself an evacuee from Burma.

Engineer Condie was efficient and intelligent.

He was well known for his persuasive power and for motivating workers to work to their optimum efficiency.

As a result, work was completed promptly.

Condie was in his 40's and had an imposing personality.

Tall.

Handsome.

Though European, he could converse in Marathi fairly well.

Seeing the workers from Kolhapur eating betelnut

leaves, he would tease them mischievously, "Kaay tamasha lavlay – what's going on?" ('Tamasha' is a popular folk dance and music of Maharashtra, and the people of Kolhapur are said to be fond of it).

The workers would respond with a smile and get back to work immediately.

And that's why the construction of the camp could be accomplished in eighteen months.

June 1943.

The special trains loaded with Polish refugees arrived at Valiwade Halt railway station.

Men and women arriving by these special trains were fair complexioned.

Six such special trains arrived.

Children, the old men and women and the widows, young men and women, formed these groups of Polish refugees.

Following them were the handicapped persons.

Most of them were rejects from the army.

The workers could see that these people were different from them.

Women wearing gowns and men in their trousers and half-sleeved shirts.

Their heads covered with hats.

Dadu Lokhande, Maruti Bhosale, Shiva Gawli, Bandu Awale, Shivappa and Gundappa, Sadhu Gawli - all of them and their families had stayed on in the camp, although the construction work was over.

They were hoping to get some work.

They extended a helping hand to the Polish refugees arriving by the special trains, by carrying their baggage.

People, alighting the trains were of the same colour and the expressions on their faces were also the same.

The expressions were of sadness, agony and the pain within.

There were no other expressions, no other emotions on their faces, not even for a fleeting moment.

The smile seemed to have vanished from their lips.

Their eyes were full of sorrow.

The innocent faces of the children appeared lost and lonely.

And the old women seemed bewildered.

It was a big crowd.

There were so many people, but hardly anyone uttered any word.

There was an occasional indistinct murmur among this long line of deportees from Poland.

Their footsteps were not brisk.

Was it a procession?

A silent protest?

Or were they going in line for a funeral?

One thing was true.

The Second World War had created history by dispossessing, dislocating these people from their homeland to an alien land, Valiwade Halt.

Poland was the first country to be attacked by Germany at the beginning of World War II, in September 1939, and two weeks later by Soviet Russia, who not only interned the Polish Forces that fell into its hands, but also deported a large number of civilian population.

Nearly two years later, the tables were turned when Russia itself was invaded by Germany and the Polish Army was then re-born in Russia.

In October 1942, due to the war situation and lack of equipment, need for convalescence and re-training, it was contemplated that part of that army be moved to India.

This was agreed, provided that the civilians, also released from Russia, were allowed to follow.

In the event the Army went to Iraq, but women with children and some disabled men came to India.

To begin with, they came from Teheran via Ahvaz to Karachi, where they were placed in a transit camp called Country Club, from where they were directed either to British East Africa or into a more permanent camp in Kolhapur.

But before the camp was built in the summer of 1943, they were moved into a temporary army camp in Malir, in the province of Sindh.

But even before this, India had agreed, in the spring of 1942, to accept about 500 Polish orphans and their guardians, directly from Russia into Balachadi Jamnagar in Gujarat.

India thus became the first country to receive Polish Refugees out of Russia during World War II.

Naturally after deprivation due to Soviet deportations, there was a general concern about recuperation of the Polish Refugees and as the hill stations were occupied by the British, the choice fell on the Deccan Plateau, namely Kolhapur, where the river Panchaganga was capable of supplying estimated 50,000 gallons of water daily.

Here, in February 1943, permission was granted by the Kolhapur Darbar, for the Polish Settlement to be built in Valiwade Park, about 4 miles east of Kolhapur on approximately 250 acres.

Unlike the Balachadi camp, located in Gujarat province at the invitation of the Maharaja of Jamnagar and at the expense of the Polish Children's Fund, subscribed to by Maharajas and the Indian firms, the building and maintenance of the Valiwade camp and its occupants was fully financed by the Polish government in exile, the money forwarded from London via the Indian Government.

Even so, the presence of the refugees caused inconvenience such as rise in prices and a draw on inadequate war-time supplies of food and other goods.

However, those things did not affect the good relations the refugees had with local people, who accepted them with grace and patience.

The building of the fully equipped Polish Refugees Camp for 5000 people, the largest in India, was completed by the end of 1943, at the cost of 32 lac rupees.

Valiwade was a little Polish village, inhabited mainly by women and children with some men relegated from the army.

It was divided into 5 districts, each consisting of 30 long barracks.

Each barrack was divided into 12 blocks of two rooms and a kitchenette; which was very important for the Polish refugees, as after years of communal life, it gave them a taste of privacy and self-sufficiency.

Along the barracks ran long verandahs and tiny garden-beds on which they decided to grow papayas, bananas and Canna flowers-their own gardens.

The Canna flower was seen a flower that gives hope and confidence.

Polish camp had its own administration with a Polish Commandant and his office, a church, a hospital, orphanage, building and repairs department, volunteer Police Force and Fire Brigade, Post Office, also a co-operative society.

Cultural and Educational department was running 4 high schools, 5 primary schools plus recreation rooms and a theatre.

They also enjoyed the contractor's cinema.

In addition to sports section, the Boy Scouts and Girl Guides movement was also thriving.

In the hot season, they camped in beautiful and cool Panhala and Chandoli.

Panhala, a hill station, was only 12 miles away.

Following the end of the Second World War and the withdrawal of recognition of the Polish government in exile, Polish Settlements in India were gradually liquidated.

ByOctober 1945, Country Club, Balachadi and Panchagani ceased to exist.

In November 1946, their inhabitants were merged into the Valiwade camp.

The Polish refugees dragged their feet into the Valiwade Halt camp through its lone gates with heavy hearts.

Thousands of feet walked on the Valiwade soil for the first time, crossing the gate.

Valiwade Halt was like a newly inhabited small township with all the amenities.

One hundred and eighty-five barracks were constructed, and each barrack had twelve blocks.

The single room and the double room blocks.

These rooms were made of concrete up to the outside verandah and were quite strong.

The walls were made of straw mats.

The Mangalore tiles formed the roof.

The distance between barracks facing each other was fifteen feet and the road between two adjacent barracks was fourteen feet wide.

There was a verandah in front, and a verandah at the back of the rooms.

A rest room and a sitting room.

Cooking was done with charcoal on individual stoves

called 'sigris.' The lighting in the camp was by means of the kerosene lamp.

The vegetable vendors formed a vegetable market on the open ground near the Camp Commandant's office.

In front of the Commandant's office was a godown, used for storing essential commodities supplied to the refugees.

The birth and death registration office was also situated here.

There was a detention room, Adjacent to it was a garden.

Honeybees were cultured here.

The Camp Commandant's office was in the first room of Barrack 1.

In the next room- number two- was the treasury room.

Paani Gravyanka, a Polish lady in her 50's was appointed as treasurer to manage the treasury room.

The camp was well equipped with facilities necessary for daily routine - an ambulance, a fire brigade jeep, a truck for garbage, a tanker and a jeep for the camp commandant.

In the north, near the railway tracks, was a kerosene depot.

Although the camp was staffed by the Polish people -administration, teachers, doctors and nurses, voluntary police, firemen etc.- there were changes in the top position of Camp Commandant.

In the first instance the Commandant was Capt. W. Jagiellowicz, who was then replaced by Lt. Col. A C B Neate, from October 1945 until January 1947, when he was followed by Lt.

Col. Diwan Singh Bhalla up to September 1947, when the position was filled by Mrs.

Mabel Button, who up to now was a Liaison Officer.

Mr. O. Grabianka was second in command to the Polish Captain – but the quartermaster in 1945 was an Indian – Mr. S. N. Rishi.

Mrs. Mabel Button lived in the Residency bungalow, facing a lake, in Kasba Bawda.

She drove to the camp in a jeep.

She made a lot of suggestions regarding the rehabilitation of the Polish refugees and supervised their implementation personally.

The inhabitants were given rooms in various barracks.

The camp Commandant's office provided essential commodities to them.

Each person was provided with a charpoy, a mattress, a bed sheet and a plate.

The secluded area, that was till recently an area of silence, was now alive with human activity.

Gradually, the daily life became a routine.

Various shops cropped up.

Soda water, bread, even the food-inns.

In order to supply the polish Camp with foodstuffs, an Indian syndicate was formed with an operational fund of Rs.1 lac.

Its managing director was Mr. Pardeshi.

The syndicate had a monopoly which was later challenged when other Indian and Polish shops were established on the other side of the Rukadi road.

The currency of transaction here were the coupons.

Printed coupons of one rupee, twelve annas, eight annas and four annas were introduced in the daily transactions.

There were coupons of one and two annas, and one and two paisa.

These coupons were limited to use only in the camp.

But the system didn't last long.

The Indian currency was brought into circulation after nine months.

When in February 1943, permission was granted by the Kolhapur Durbar to locate the Polish camp in Valivade, it was on the understanding that the Kolhapur state will get a greater allocation of food.

This did not happen, and it became a source of recrimination for the Local Authorities against the camp.

Naturally an injection of even such a small foreign body into local population gave rise to inflation - 50% as against 25% national average, and certain food shortages in the later part of the camp's existence.

It is with this background that certain rationing was introduced and coupons were contemplated.

It is also worth noting that there was a famine in Bengal in 1943, kept secret by the British, and a failed harvest in Punjab in 1946.

The arrangement of fire brigade was amazing.

An iron angle was hung at the corner of every barrack.

In the event of fire, the iron angle was struck.

The people hearing it in the next barrack would also strike the iron angle at the corner of their barrack.

This is how the message of the spreading of fire reached the fire brigade through the beating of the iron-angle at the corner of every barrack.

A watch tower had been built on a hill in the centre of the camp.

The tower made of wood, was fifty feet in height.

A vigilant policeman was stationed on top of it, round the clock, to keep a watch over the camp and in any eventuality of fire, the policeman would spot the location of fire and instruct the fire brigade to move in that direction.

In those days, the water pipes available were short.

So the distance between the place on fire and the fire brigade could not be covered with a single pipe.

Short lengths of pipes were joined together, without losing much time, to create a long pipe and the fire would then be brought under control and extinguished with an enormous flow of water.

The water for dousing the blaze was supplied from the numerous tanks, but the pumps were mainly hand-operated.

The central tank was in the middle of the camp.

In the south of the camp was built a large tank, to supply water to the entire camp.

Water was supplied through taps.

One pipe would have minimum six and maximum twelve taps attached to it.

This supply was used as drinking water.

In the east of the tank were bath enclosures.

One for men, the other for women.

These public bath enclosures were equipped with showers.

About three hundred men and women could have bath at the same time.

Large stone platforms were made for washing clothes with separate taps, outside bath enclosures.

The narrow strips of soil alongside the bamboo blocks soon became tiny but colourful gardens.

Long verandahs were blooming with lush greenery.

Due to war shortages and the intended temporary nature of the transit camp, the buildings were rather primitive, but were new and clean.

What was more important, they were no longer communal.

They gave privacy to the inhabitants.

For the Polish refugees, it was an indescribable joy – to be able to shut the door and be alone, unsupervised, nor spied on.

And what a pleasure to cook in one's own kitchen.

Every house was given a spear, two buckets and a spray pump as a fire extinguisher.

The camp had a rule that the two buckets must always be full of water.

Every family was given allowance money by the government through the camp Commandant's office.

From the allowance money received, they had to feed and clothe themselves.

The buildings, water and schools were provided free.

The monthly allowance was: for adults and teenagers Rs.43.48 paise + Rs.10 as pocket money; for children of 12 years: Rs.45, for 6 year-old Rs. 28, and below 6 years Rs. 25.

The average daily cost of food was Rs. 2.16 paise for an adult and Rs1.48 for a child.

In the beginning, the hostel was entrusted with the catering management.

Pan Paluch, in his 50's and Ogibinski in his 60's were given the charge as managers to oversee the catering arrangement.

There was a great demand not only for wheat bread but also for potatoes.

Mutton was not very popular. pan Paluch and pan Ogibinski were involved in a Co-operative (spoldzielnia) called "zgoda" (Harmony) which ran various workshops, including a cafeteria.

They were given food for the first two days after arriving in the camp.

After that they had to cater for themselves except

for the patients in hospital and the orphanage where pan Klecki worked as a quartermaster.

A fellow called Maruti, despite not knowing any Polish worked on printing their newspaper.

Another one that knew all their names was Salokhe who ran the Indian Post Office in the camp.

The street hawkers who learned the Polish names of the wares so well, that if you did not see their faces, a mistake could be made, thinking they were Polish.

The nine-year old Dadu Lokhande, the boy from the neighboring Valiwade village, joined pan Klecki as office boy on a monthly salary of ten rupees.

The eighteen-year old Maruti Dashrath Bhosale got the job as a worker in the hostel situated in barrack 114.

Bandu Hari Awale started working as a sweeper in the camp at Rs. 15 a month.

There were other locals who got jobs in the sanitary department.

Shiva, Sadhu Gawli, Hegde and others.

Maruti Bhosale's father was a cook in children's orphanage.

Five Polish women assisted him in cooking.

There were about 400 children in the orphanage on Valiwade road.

Fortunately, for Dadu Lokhande, the children were not exactly infants.

All of them were over 4 years.

They could manage the basic activities on their own.

The sight of these orphaned, innocent children created turmoil in the observer's heart.

They had nobody to love them, or to take them on their lap, or to hug them with affection, or to give a warm kiss on their cheeks.

But they survived the lack of love and attention.

Nature taught them survival.

Their innocent faces wouldn't have been seen, if Poland were turned into Hiroshima.

Poland to Hindusthan.......

Those were endless journeys - by horse carriage, on raft or on foot, Through the Russian stops, by overcrowded unseaworthy boats from Krasnowdsk to Pahlavi, or in trucks across the Persian mountains, then tents in Tehran, or stables in Ahwaz, long ship travel along the Persian Gulf and Indian Ocean, more tents and barracks in the transit camp near Karachi.

And then India – to Valiwade.

These children and the other inhabitants of the camp had travelled thousands of miles.

But they seemed immune to joy as well as sorrow.

But how would the big leaders of the big nations understand the innocence in the eyes of these little children?

How?

The disarming smiles on these faces could not prevent the overambitious leaders in their scramble for power.

They forced endless atrocities and agony on these exiled children.

The dazed, lost look on their faces gradually gave way to their instinctive nature.

Some children in the camp and the orphanage started misbehaving and playing pranks on others.

They were sent straight away to the remand home like Borstal school.

The life in the refugee camp became a routine...but not everybody liked living a routine life.

Lady Burton had established her authority in the camp.

That's why nobody except the Poles were allowed into the camp.

The workers like Bhosale, Gawli, Lokhande, Hegde had to wear a badge for their identification.

There was a strict rule that everybody had to return to the camp latest by eight in the evening.

Those who came late were issued warnings.

And if the warnings didn't work, the latecomers were sent to the detention room in the camp.

Besides the naughty children, there were women who liked to roam around.

A lot of them went for a stroll on the Kolhapur road to Shri Jaggad Guru monastery.

They would go to Kolhapur by the morning eight or the eleven o'clock train.

Rarely would they go to Kolhapur by the evening five o'clock train.

The return trains from Kolhapur to Miraj were at nine in the morning, twelve noon and then the last train was at eight in the evening.

Everything was available in the camp, prompting some Poles to put up shops right in the camp.

The 45 year pan Piorkowski started a sodawater-cold drinks shop.

The 55-year old pan Szustek started selling cakes.

The women from the nearby villages like Valiwade, Chinchwad would sell vegetables in the camp.

Language was a major barrier to communicate with each other.

So sometimes they would get one rupee for vegetables worth one anna.

When a woman raised one finger, the Poles didn't understand whether she meant one anna or one rupee.

There were more women than men in the camp.

The constant fights among women were instrumental in making the camp all the more lively.

The chatter among the women was never-ending.

The intensity of their sorrow decreased as time passed.

More because of their playful nature. pan Lipinski living in Barrack 23 was known in the entire camp for his sense of humour and was called a joker.

He was about 48 and served as an officer in his country's army.

He was six feet tall.

There was a hole in his throat.

And a rubber tube was placed in it.

He could speak only after closing the hole of the rubber tube with his palm.

He was huge and hefty.

Very often, he would lift Maruti Bhosale and Dadu Lokhande simultaneously with his hands.

He could lift anything weighing 60-70 kilos in a second and carry it over his back as if it were straw.

The other source of their entertainment was different games like table tennis, volleyball and football.

The football matches were played every Sunday on the open ground near Kolhapur road.

The Vadgaon team had defeated the Polish team twice in these matches.

The Chhatrapati park in Barrack 158 was converted into a Church.

There was a hall adjacent to the Church.

The performances of dance and music programmes began here.

The young men and women in their twenties took part in these performances.

The old men and women spent their time in the church.

Cinema made an entry into the camp.

Pardeshi of Kolhapur erected a tent just outside the camp.

English films like 'Thief of Baghdad', 'Tarzan' were shown here.

Once in a while, Hindi-Marathi films like 'Sant Dnyaneshwar', 'Sant Tukaram', 'Khazanchi' and 'Shezari' were also shown here.

Out of curiosity, the Poles watched the Hindi, Marathi films.

The schools responded to the appeal from the Polish Red Cross in Bombay to write letters to the Polish soldiers.

Some of these soldiers were not able to trace members of their families.

They felt lonely and lost.

A sergeant delivered the post to the residents of Polish camps every morning.

He would ask, "Would you like to write a letter to an unknown soldier?" Marian Kurzawski, a cadet in the Airman School in Heliopolis received letters from her mother and sister in India, but she liked to correspond.

So she took two.

One from a Polish girl in Africa and the other from Mita Turowicz in India.

Mita was a friend of her sister Alina.

That was an interesting coincidence.

During their correspondence, one of Mita's letters, written on a handmade Chrismas Card and also signed by Alina, instead of going to Marian's school in Egypt, went to the military hospital in Scotland.

It was here in the hospital in Scotland that Marian

and Alina Kurzawski's father, Jan Kurzawski, received the letter.

At the time, Jan Kurzawski had no knowledge of the whereabouts of his family.

The unexpected letter was happy news for him.

He got to learn about his daughters Marian and Alina, through an unexpected, misdirected letter.

Truth is, indeed, stranger than fiction.

Chapter 21

The Polish Boys Who Cycled to Goa

The refugee camp at Valivade shimmered under a molten sky.

Tin Roofs crackled; dust clung to everything.

Among the five thousand Poles who had escaped Siberian exile and the chaos of war, a restless energy simmered.

Around a crude hand-drawn map, a group of Polish Boy Scouts plotted what sounded like madness.

"Goa," said fifteen-year-old Kazik, tracing a finger across the page.

"The tomb of St. Francis Xavier.

We'll go there by bicycle." "Easy," quipped Marek, the camp joker.

"You can't even ride to the kitchen without collapsing." Janek, small and sharp-eyed, grinned.

"If St. Francis could cross oceans, we can cross India." When Father A.

Jankowski, their chaplain, heard the plan, he nearly spilled his tea.

"You're out of your minds," he told them.

"It's two hundred and fifty miles of heat, hills, and potholes." "Then God will pedal with us," Marek said solemnly — to everyone's delight.

And so, with patched-up bicycles, paper maps, and youthful conviction, the boys set out to prove that faith could roll on two wheels.

At dawn, twenty-four bicycles clattered out of the camp gates.

The entire settlement turned out to cheer them on — waving handkerchiefs, shouting blessings in Polish and Marathi, dogs barking in chorus.

The boys pedalled south through dry villages and waving sugarcane, singing Polish scout songs that echoed down the dusty road.

By noon, the Deccan sun was merciless.

Water boiled in their flasks.

Shirts stiffened with salt.

When one boy's chain snapped, the others stopped to fix it with a shoelace and a prayer.

When another fainted dramatically by the roadside, they revived him with mangoes and laughter.

They traded songs for fruit in the villages they passed.

Curious locals gathered to stare at this strange procession — tanned, smiling, half-burnt boys on rickety bicycles, flying the invisible flag of a homeland far away.

"They came like a miracle," a farmer later said.

"Sunburned and singing, their wheels shimmering in the dust." That night, they camped under a banyan tree, sharing the last of their biscuits.

Fireflies blinked like distant candles.

In his diary, Father Jankowski wrote: "They have no sense of fear, only of direction.

Perhaps that is what faith truly means." Beyond Belgaum, the road tilted upward into the misty folds of the Western Ghats.

The air turned cool, the land green and steep.

"Behold," announced Marek, staring at the hills.

"The staircase to heaven." "Or to hospital," muttered Kazik.

The climb was punishing.

Tyres slipped on red mud; sweat ran like rivers.

When rain swept in, they shouted with joy and raced through waterfalls, laughing like wild saints.

A monkey stole their bananas.

A bee stung Father Jankowski, who muttered, "I see now why St. Francis preferred boats." At night, soaked to the bone, they built smoky fires under trees.

Marek performed imitations of their priest balancing on an imaginary bicycle, swinging a censer.

Even Father Jankowski laughed till he cried.

By day, they pushed through jungle fog and mountain silence.

They named every bend after a Polish city — Warsaw Bend, Kraków Corner, Lwów Hill — remapping exile into memory.

"Downhill to Goa!" someone shouted as they began the final descent.

"If we survive this, I'm canonizing my bicycle!" After seven days of blazing sun, monsoon rain, and endless hills, the scent of salt filled the air.

And there it was — the Arabian Sea, blue and infinite.

They whooped, rang their bicycle bells, and plunged into the waves in full uniform, their laughter rolling over the surf.

On May 8, 1943, twenty-four Polish boys cycled into Panjim — sun-browned, blistered, but radiant.

Local Portuguese scouts ran alongside them, cheering.

Newspapers called it "a miracle on wheels." That evening, at a small reception, a man in a white linen suit approached.

"I am Don Vasco da Gama," he said with a gentle smile.

"A descendant of the admiral who discovered India." Marek leaned toward Janek and whispered, "Does he also have a flat tyre?" Even the priest failed to keep a straight face.

The next moning, they stood inside the Basilica of Bom Jesus, before the silver casket of St.

Francis Xavier.

Incense swirled.

Sunlight streamed through high windows.

Their voices rose in trembling unison: "Święty Franciszku Ksawery, módl się za nami." Saint Francis Xavier, pray for us.

Janek knelt, awed.

"He looks alive," he whispered.

"Like he's listening." When the Mass ended, the boys made a daring request — a relic to take home.

The priests could not grant it.

Instead, they gave them a white ribbon that had adorned the saint's tomb for a decade.

It wasn't gold or bone — just a strip of faith.

The boys tied it to a handlebar, and as they rode through Panjim, it fluttered like a flag for a country that existed only in memory.

Their pilgrimage didn't end at the basilica.

Invited by Goan scouts, they cycled to Bambolim Beach, where palms leaned toward the sea.

There they built a tiny chapel from seashells and driftwood — each shell glinting like a prayer in sunlight.

At night, they sat by the fire as waves hissed against the sand.

Father Jankowski read aloud from a weathered history book: "There was once another Pole here — Gaspar da Gama, a Jew from Poland who guided the Portuguese explorers to Goa." Marek smiled.

"Then we're not the first Poles in Goa," he said.

"Just the first ones with bicycles." Laughter rippled into the night, carried away by the wind.

Months later, back in Valivade, the boys gathered in the small camp cemetery for All Souls' Day.

Their bicycles leaned nearby, the white ribbon still tied to one handlebar, faint and frayed but unbroken.

"You have carried our homeland across mountains and rivers," said Father Jankowski softly.

"And though we are far from Poland, she lives wherever you keep the light burning." The candles flickered.

Somewhere in the dusk, a bicycle bell chimed — faint, familiar, eternal.

Janek smiled.

"Guess St.

Francis liked the ride," he said.

The others laughed — and for a moment, under that Indian sky, exile itself felt conquered.

Because no homeland is lost when memory still moves — even on two dusty wheels "They had no flag, no army, no country — but they made Poland visible again, on bicycles." — Father A.

Jankowski

Chapter 22

The School with No Country

The blackboard was scratched.
The desks were mismatched.
The textbooks were secondhand, borrowed or translated, sometimes handwritten from memory.
But the laughter?
That was unmistakably Polish.
So was the discipline.
So was the hope.
In the heart of Maharashtra, among mango trees and monsoon mud, there stood a school with no country—a Polish high school in exile, built from ruins of war and fragments of stolen childhoods.
Its students had survived Siberian labor camps, hunger, disease, and the shattering knowledge that they might never see home again.
But inside those classrooms, something profound happened: They began to dream again.
The Polish Settlement at Valivade, near Kolhapur, wasn't a village by accident—it was designed to be a miniature republic.
A place where displaced Poles could live not merely as refugees, but as a community in exile.
It had its own church, shops, scouting organizations, bakeries—and at the centre of it all, its school.
There, under the relentless Indian sun, students

recited Mickiewicz, wrote essays on Sienkiewicz, and calculated geometry problems in Polish.

The school followed a curriculum crafted to mimic what they would have studied in Warsaw or Kraków, had their lives not been broken by war and deportation.

There were biology classes, chemistry taught from old equipment, and literature read aloud with reverence.

The teachers were often survivors themselves—former professors, librarians, nurses—people who had once been forced to dig trenches in Kazakhstan, now resurrected as educators and guardians of the nation's soul.

They wore pressed white shirts.

Some had neckties made from curtain scraps.

Their shoes were polished, even if worn thin.

The 1943 graduating class stood in rows under a makeshift canopy, their hearts bursting not just with pride, but disbelief.

They had made it.

Wiesia Kleszko, whose name would later appear in memoirs and letters, stood with her peers—many of whom had arrived in India barely able to walk, haunted by the ghosts of Soviet prisons or orphaned by famine.

And yet, here they were: high school graduates, speaking fluent Polish, reciting poetry, applying to universities abroad.

"We didn't just study history," she said years later.

"We were living proof that history could not erase us." But the schoolyard held shadows, too.

Every classroom had its absences—students who had succumbed to illness, despair, or the lingering effects of Soviet camps.

Some names were spoken quietly.

Others were not spoken at all.

But none were forgotten.

"One of our classmates," Wiesia remembered, "was a quiet boy of 29.

He had longed to finish his education, but his body, already worn down from deportation, couldn't hold on.

He died just six months after his final exams." Another, only 20, died from bone tuberculosis despite multiple surgeries and the best care Indian doctors could offer.

In a place where families had been torn apart, the school became a surrogate family, and the students became mourners, caretakers, torchbearers.

Each week, the flag was raised.

It was a battered piece of cloth—red and white—stitched and restitched a dozen times.

But to the students, it was as sacred as a relic.

They sang the national anthem not because they were told to, but because it called something sacred out of them—something primal and unbreakable.

The land beneath their feet was Indian, the food on their plates was Indian, but the language of their hearts remained Polish.

"Jeszcze Polska nie zginęła…" "Poland is not yet lost…" The words rang across the settlement, over the mango orchards, through the barracks, and into the sky, where they mingled with birdsong and incense.

The school wasn't just for children.

Evenings saw adults gathering to attend night classes—in English, carpentry, sewing, agriculture, even accounting.

War had robbed many of their professions.

Now, they sought to rebuild not only knowledge, but dignity.

One former landowner from Lwów became a math tutor.

A violinist taught music from memory.

A nun taught art using crushed flowers for paint.

This wasn't education—it was resurrection.

Though separated by language and religion, the Poles and Indians found subtle ways to connect.

Indian teachers and doctors, intrigued by the passionate energy of this little Poland-in-exile, sometimes volunteered to teach or offer supplies.

Locals attended school plays and Polish concerts with wide eyes and open arms.

One Indian boy, fascinated by the Polish students, used to sit outside the fence and listen to lessons.

He learned to write his name in Polish before he knew how to do so in Marathi.

There were moments of shared joy: cricket matches played with sticks and laughter.

Shared sweets during Diwali.

Easter eggs exchanged for strings of jasmine.

The warmth of India softened exile.

As 1948 approached, the writing was on the wall.

The camp would not last forever.

Some students would leave for England, some to Australia, some back to a broken and Soviet-dominated Poland.

Others would remain in India longer, waiting for visas, family, or clarity.

On the last day of school, no one spoke for a while after the final bell rang.

The students walked slowly, as if trying to memorize each step.

Some touched the desks one last time.

Others folded notes and buried them in the ground—a time capsule of exile, hope, and longing.

One girl left a poem under a loose floorboard.

It read: "If the wind carries my words to Poland, Tell her I never forgot the smell of her earth.

Even here, in mango lands, I sang your name Every morning like a prayer." Though Poland was far—occupied, divided, and bruised—the Polish School in Valivade proved one thing beyond doubt: A nation can exist without borders, without government, even without soil——so long as it lives in language, memory, and the fierce conviction of its children.

And so, the classrooms emptied.

The flag was folded.

The chalkboards were wiped clean one last time.

But in every student's heart, the lessons burned bright: Home is not a place.

It is a promise.

Chapter 23

Every night, at midnight

No screams.
No shouts.
No whispers.
Just nothing.
Even the cats and dogs in the camp had perceived that they were not to meow or bark or whimper at that time.

This silence was only for a few minutes because at this hour, the Poles would hold their breath and stay glued to the radio to hear the B.B.C. news.

Implied in the news was the information that was to determine the future of these refugees.

Contacts with the local people were not very easy.

The greatest difficulty was the language.

They were beginning to learn English.

Only a few of them managed to learn some words of Marathi.

There was also the fact that India was then a part of the British Empire.

The British liaison officers didn't encourage socializing between the Poles and the locals.

But they managed to overcome it.

The children did it first.

The Polish Boy Scouts had very friendly relations with the Indian Boy Scouts from Kolhapur.

Their Commissioner, D.M. Valivadekar was a frequent visitor to the camp.

They also visited a scout centre in the nearby Rukadi.

For English lessons, they had to depend on Indian teachers.

Some Indian children learnt Polish quite easily.

So did the Indian postmaster in Valiwade.

Her Highness the Maharani of Kolhapur visited the camp once with her two children.

And when the new Maharaja of Kolhapur was crowned, the Polish Boy Scouts and Girl Guides were invited to take part in the coronation parade.

While camping in Panahala, the nearby hill station, they were allowed to visit Maharani's palace and were occasionally sent some delicacies.

On the other hand, when camping in Chandoli, much further afield, the local Indian women would bring their sick children to the Polish camp for medicine and help.

It was five years since they had settled down in the Valiwade camp.

Their relations with the local people had strengthened.

A lot of people from Kolhapur visited the camp.

Some of them had developed relations with the Polish girls here.

Some relations turned into serious alliances.

Kashikar and Pardeshi married Polish girls.

The war ended in 1945.

By the Yalta agreements, Poland and the Rest of Eastern Europe was left under the Communist rule of Russia.

The Allies ceased to recognise the Polish Government in London, which paid for them during the war.

United Nations' 'Relief and Rehabilitation

Administration – UNRRA, took over the care of the camps in India.

The government issued the orders of their return to their homeland.

Only 473 people, out of the 5000, decided to return to Poland.

The rest mostly chose to sail to England, some to East Africa, a small number to Lebanon.

They were to sail in ships to their destinations.

The Polish refugees gradually started preparing for the return to their homeland.

The preparations were over, the baggage was ready.

And finally the time arrived to bid farewell to the local friends. pan Klecki called Dadu, "Chodz tutaj - Come here" Dadu, busy in his work, came and greeted him in Polish.

"Dzien dobry" "Co chcesz? - what would you like to have ?" pan Klecki asked him.

Dadu said nothing.

He just stood speechless. pan Klecki removed his wrist watch and with a big smile on his face and affection in his eyes, he gifted the watch to Dadu.

Dadu was deeply touched by his gesture. pan Klecki said to him, "Pamietaj o mnie - don't ever forget me" The barracks in the camp began to be vacated.

A feel of emptiness engulfed the entire camp.

Hordes of Polish people were vacating their hitherto lively barracks. pani Yanka had nobody.

She was all alone.

Dashrath picked up her bag and carried it over his head. pani Yanka and Dashrath started walking on the road to the railway station.

They exchanged a few words while walking.

"Boze, tak bardzo sie tutaj meczylem.

Mam juz tego dosyc.- By God I've suffered a lot. I'm really fed up now," pani Yanka expressed her agony.

"Co robic, wola boska. - what can one do if God wills it," Dashrath tried to console her.

Their steps towards the station were slow.

They knew that the train would not leave until everybody had boarded it.

In the meantime, Dashrath's youngest son, Vasant came running to them.

Dashrath asked his son to greet pani Yanka.

He joined his hands doing Namaskar, greeting her.

"Arrey Vashya, say do baravature." The boy could not say anything. pani Yanka was carrying a sweater in her hand.

Giving it to the boy she said to Dashrath, "Cholpiec jest bardzo madry, trzeba go uczyc. - He is a smart boy.

Get him good education." pan Szustek had given away his tables and chairs to Sadhu Gawli.

He advised him not to drink too much, "Uwazaj na siebie - take care of yourself" Gawli was overwhelmed and was touched by his advice.

"Pilnuj dzieci, sa takie male - Take care of your children, they are very young." The special train was already there at Valiwade Halt station.

Most of the Poles had left by earlier specials.

This was the last special.

More than the joy of returning to their homeland was the sorrow and the agony of living as refugees for some years.

Their countenance embodied all the years of pain and suffering into an ice-berg like serenity.

The anxiety of the future was knawing at their hearts within.

It was going to be a return to their homeland, to their own soil or to a new land of their choice, to create a new world all over again.

The only ray of happiness was that the war was over.

The workers here would never see these faces ever again.

These faces had become a part of their lives. pan Priokowski who sold soda water, clerk pan Asha working in the Commandant's office, baker pan Susto, the ever smiling affectionate pan Lipinski, pani Anka, pani Hela, pani Staslia - all these faces were to disappear from the sky that covered this exuberant camp.

There was nobody on the railway platform except the workers.

All the Poles had boarded the train.

As pan Lipinski shouted loudly from the compartment calling Bandu Awale, the whistle of the engine filled the atmosphere signalling the departure of the train.

The train moved.

Lipinski picked up his coat and threw it in the direction of Bandu who caught hold of it.

Lipinski was saying, "Jade teraz do mojej ojczyzny - I'm going to my motherland" Waving her hand from the window, pan Asha was bidding farewell, "Jedziemy, Jedziemy dowidzenia, dowidzenia........ - we are going, we are going, goodbye, Goodbye...."

Chapter 24

The Polish camp

The Polish camp that had the buzz of the blue and green eyes continued to have the existence of the same blue and green eyes, though there weren't any Polish refugees in the camp.

The only difference was that the eyes were neither of innocent children nor of young women.

They were the eyes of cats and dogs that were left behind by the Poles.

Between 1943-48, Valiwade was a little Polish village inhabited mainly by women and children with some men relegated from the army.

They were the deportees from Poland as a consequence of the Second World War.

The endless babble and chatter had vanished.

All that could be heard now was the feeble barking of the dogs and the languish mewing of the cats.

The giggles, the guffaws and the prittle- prattle appeared to be alien emotions to the Valiwade camp.

The rainbow of colours kissed the sky in the morning sun as usual but it appeared lacklustre and gloomy.

The soft sunrays shrouded the camp but they too seemed subdued.

All the activity had come to a halt.

The shops remained closed.

The school bell did not ring anymore.

There wasn't any movement on the streets.

The rustic women carrying vegetable baskets stopped coming to the solitary camp.

Everything had frozen to stillness and a hushed silence.

So dull, so isolated.

Dadoba Lokhande, Maruti Bhosale were worried.

How do they earn their livelihood?

They feared being dissipated in this godforsaken place.

But Bandu Avale, Shiva Gavli, and Ganpat Hegde, had a faint hope that one more special train would arrive.

One more special.

Man lives on hope.

So did their families.

Gradually, that hope began waning.

They had to do something to earn their living.

Seeing the agitated and hungry faces of their women and children would sink their hearts.

At last, Maruti Bhosale decided to leave for his village, Herle, about fifteen miles west of Valiwade camp.

Bandu Avale took the same decision.

Packing up bag and baggage, they turned on the way to their village .

Only Hegde and Gavli stayed on in the camp.

Days went by.

The government released a statement.

It had spent a lot of money on the camp that was now desolated.

Nobody was there to take care of it and maintain it.

The camp was orphaned.

The government had decided to send a special train to the camp.

The news rekindled the hopes of Hegde, Gavli and their families.

They felt a sense of relief but wished Maruti and Dadoba had not left the camp, feeling sorry for them.

The year was 1949 and India had got freedom from the British rule.

Therefore, the expectations were high that the special train would bring something special.

And finally a special arrived, but it was a special jammed with men in green military uniform.

They were soldiers.

The soldiers, caged in the compartments, jumped down the train one after another stretching their arms, exercising their legs, they shrugged off the fatigue of travelling in the packed train.

The loud sound of the heavy iron-trunks thrown to the ground merged with the sound of the heels of their boots hitting the ground hard.

These sounds fell on the ears of Hegde and Gavli.

Their hopes had faded again.

Maybe, the next special would bring in something for their livelihood.

But this was the last special.

No other special arrived after this one.

The special train had brought soldiers especially to take care of the camp.

The soldiers were to look after everything.

Consequently, no outsiders would get any work here.

Despite it, Hegde and others felt that they could earn something by doing some errands for the soldiers.

There were five thousand Poles living here.

The total battalion consisted of only six hundred soldiers who lived a regimented time-bound life.

There wasn't anything new to experience beyond their disciplined routine.

Major Misal was the camp commandant.

He was moved by the plight of the three families.

He gave them some errands to help them make the two ends meet.

Two years passed. 1950.

India, now a free country, had faced the trauma of partition.

There was an exodus of refugees coming from the newly created Pakistan.

The government had earmarked camps for their rehabilitation.

Valiwade was one of them.

Quite a few specials were expected.

At least two thousand refugees were scheduled to arrive.

Chhatrapati Rajaram Maharaj, the King of Kolhapur, had arranged for their meals.

The King's cooks had prepared meals for the exodus of refugees.

But the preparations were in vain.

The special did not arrive on the scheduled day.

They did finally arrive.

Three thousand refugees from Sindh.

Shashi Gajwani took a deep breath remembering the amazing Polish Refugee Camp in Valivade where his family, along with three thousand Sindhi refugees were rehabilitated after the Partition of India in 1947.

Bajo Gajwani

Chapter 25

The Night of No Fear

Bajo stood still in the dim light of the Kolhapur street, facing the three boys whose anger cracked and sizzled like lightning without rain.

Yet even in that tense moment, his mind traveled—not in panic, but in memory.

He was not standing here alone.

He was standing with Sindh behind him.

The wide, slow swell of the Sindhu River shimmered in his thoughts—its waters golden at dawn, silver at dusk.

As a child, he would sit on its banks for hours, his bare feet dipped in the silt-rich water, the lap of waves soft as a lullaby.

The air there always smelled faintly of wet earth, turmeric, and temple incense.

There was a rhythm to life along the Sindhu—a calm, unhurried breath that even time seemed to follow.

He remembered his mother, Paari, her hands always busy but her eyes always gentle.

The sound of her bangles as she kneaded dough.

The warm aroma of phulkas puffing over a clay chulha.

Her voice humming old Sindhi folk songs: " Nangra nimaani da jeevein teevein paalna…" Songs that spoke of devotion, love and resilience.

His father, Parchomal, was a man of few words.

But every morning he would rise before the sun, open the shutters of his shop, and swept the front steps himself.

He taught Bajo by action, not lecture: dignity was not something you asked for—it was something you quietly upheld, even when no one was looking.

And Bakhat, his grandmother—her laughter was dry like the desert winds, but her faith was as deep as the river.

She told stories of Sindh's old saints, of Jhulelal, the protector of their people, whose spirit, she said, lived in the very waters of the Indus.

She'd sit on the charpai under the neem tree, the scent of cardamom tea swirling in the air, telling Bajo: " Zindagi mein sab kujh chhinnji saghetho, lekin hika gaalih na...izzat..panhinji izzat...panhinje hatha mein aahe.." ("Everything in life can be taken, except one thing—your dignity, which is always in your own hands.") Jadalmal, his grandfather, was a hard worker and never stopped working .

He lit diyas with the reverence of one who understood that the divine lives not only in shrines, but in every small act of kindness.

Bajo could still hear the crisp rustle of the neem leaves above the temple, smell the ghee from the flickering lamps, see the soft glow of twilight on his grandfather's lined face.

Then came Partition.

The river had watched silently as their world burned.

Bajo remembered—he would never forget—the terror of the crossing.

How his family carried only what they could fit into cloth bundles.

How the riverside was thick with the stench of smoke, blood, and bodies.

How his mother, even then, never let go of his hand.

And yet—despite the horror, he also remembered the dignity with which his parents and grandparents held themselves.

In the refugee camps, where the nights were cold and the food was scarce, they shared what little they had.

His mother still sang.

His father still rose at dawn.

This—this—was the soil Bajo came from.

He looked into the eyes of the boy standing in front of him now.

The boy's breath was ragged.

His fists clenched.

But Bajo saw through the bravado: fear, hunger, helplessness.

The same ghosts that had once shadowed his own people.

" Maan Sindhu jo waaris aahyaan.

Maiin Sindhu ka beta hoon,..I am an inheritor of Sindhu." Bajo said softly, switching to the purest Sindhi for a moment without realizing.

Then, in Hindi, steady: "I was born by the Sindhu River.

I have seen everything—the rise, the fall, the loss.

But we never lost ourselves.

My family taught me: no one can make you smaller unless you let them." The drizzle brushed his skin.

The night air smelled of wet stone, but in his mind, he smelled the Indus waters again—fresh and eternal.

The leader of the boys shifted, his anger slowly unravelling.

Bajo's voice dropped lower.

"We were called outsiders there.

We are called outsiders here.

But we have only carried one thing with us—respect. For ourselves, and for others.

That is what we were taught on the banks of Sindhu." He paused, the quiet around them deepening.

Even the wind seemed to listen.

"Maarna hai toh maar lo," he said, calm as the river.

"Par yaad rakhna—main un logon ka beta hoon jinhone sab kuch khona seekh liya, lekin apni khuddari kabhi nahi chhodi." ("If you must, then beat me. But remember—I am the son of people who learned to lose everything but never let go of their self-respect") The leader's eyes darted away.

The youngest boy blinked, his shoulders sagging slightly.

A moment later, the leader muttered, "Jaa...go.." And so Bajo walked on, the rain kissing his face.

But as he moved, he carried with him not fear, but the wide sky of Sindh, the sacred Sindhu river, and the voices of his ancestors—whispering not of hatred, but of endurance, grace, and unbreakable spirit.

Chapter 26

Friendship and Fizz in Valivade

After Partition, Valivade, near Kolhapur, was more than a refugee camp — it was a testament to human endurance.

What had begun as a temporary settlement grew into a living township, vibrant and self-sustaining.

Its offshoot, Gandhinagar Colony, remains alive even today — a thriving reminder that new life can grow from displacement.

For those who lived through those early years, Valivade was a landscape of courage and laughter.

Between the barracks of brick and cement, people rebuilt families, livelihoods, and small joys.

Among the hum of sewing machines and the clang of tin trunks, there was also the sparkle of glass bottles — and, for one boy named SG, the laughter of his closest friend, Arjun Prabhdas Makhija.

Their friendship — and the little universe around Shabban's Colddrink Shop — came to define the golden afternoons of Valivade.

Valivade's barracks stood in long, straight rows — strong walls of brick and cement roofed with red mangalore tiles that glimmered under the sun.

Between them ran narrow, lively lanes where every sound — a child's laughter, a cycle bell, a street vendor's call — carried the rhythm of a community alive and rebuilding.

At the start of Barrack 13 stood a shop known to every resident — Jotu Pasaari's Grocery.

The first house of the row was a world of sacks, scales, and stories.

Jotu Pasaari, the patriarch, ran it with firm kindness, aided by his son Prabhdas and his grandsons — Kanhaiya, Lalu, and the youngest, Arjun.

Customers streamed in all day — mothers weighing out rice, children asking for a handful of sugar crystals, men collecting kerosene or dal.

The air smelled of gur, soap, and roasted grain.

And in the middle of it all, Arjun darted about, his boyish energy contagious, his laughter the soundtrack of the shop.

He was the grandson of the great Jotu Pasaari — a family name spoken with affection and respect.

To SG, Arjun was more than a friend; he was a part of Valivade's living heartbeat.

When SG's family moved to Kolhapur city, life changed.

St. Xavier's High School was a different world — tiled classrooms, polished shoes, and teachers who spoke of progress and possibility.

But the camp never really left him.

Once or twice a month, SG would return to Valivade — walking past the fields and railway line until the familiar outlines of the barracks rose against the horizon.

The very air there smelled of childhood: dust, food, smoke, and the faint sweetness of syrup from Shabban's Colddrink Shop.

Waiting at the gate, as always, would be Arjun — sleeves rolled up, hair tousled, grin ready.

Their destination never changed.

Shabban's shop stood in the long row of small stores nestled on the long street between the row of barracks.

The wooden counter, polished by countless hands, was fronted by benches where customers sat, sipping slowly, letting the fizz tickle their noses.

Behind the counter stood Shabban himself — round-faced, soft-spoken, with a smile that made everyone feel at home.

He had kind eyes, always saying something pleasant: "Arjun, aju ji soda masstt aahe, taazi and mazzedaar ......Arjun, today's soda is the best — fresh from the siphon!" But the true magic lay in how he made his drinks.

Shabban's workspace was modest but full of wonder.

Against the wall sat heavy glass bottles — thick, green-tinted, built to hold pressure.

Beside them were two soda siphons, large steel cylinders with brass fittings, attached to a hand-pump.

On one side stood glass jars of his homemade syrups — lemon, orange, rose, pineapple, and jeera — glowing like jewels in the light.

Each morning, Shabban mixed sugar, water, and natural essence in a large aluminum dekchi over a coal stove.

The syrup simmered gently, filling the lane with the scent of citrus and spice.

Once cooled, it was strained through muslin and stored in glass jars, sealed with wax paper and a twine knot.

That was Shabban's secret — everything made fresh, nothing from a bottle.

When Arjun and SG arrived, Shabban's eyes lit up.

"Two lemon sodas, extra fizz?" he'd ask, though he already knew the answer.

He'd pour a spoonful of syrup into a tall glass, add a twist of lime, a pinch of salt, and then — with a little flourish — release a stream of soda from the siphon.

The sound was a thrill: hissss-shhh! as the carbonated water danced and frothed, tiny bubbles rising like laughter itself.

He'd stir it briskly with a long-handled spoon, then slide the glasses across the counter, the rims beaded with condensation.

The first sip always made SG's eyes widen.

It was sharp and cool, the lemon biting just enough before the sweetness caught up.

The fizz rose through his throat and made him laugh every single time.

"This," he'd say, "is happiness in a glass." Sometimes they tried other flavours — rose pink as dawn, orange bright as sunset, pineapple golden and sweet.

But nothing ever matched the tang of soda lemon, that perfect blend of sparkle and simplicity. "Someday," SG mused once, "someone will make a drink like this and sell it all over India." Arjun chuckled.

"Then they'll call it Shabban's Special — and we'll drink for free forever." Years later, when Limca arrived in the market — bottled, branded, and advertised — SG smiled at the memory.

Limca was crisp, yes, but it lacked something.

It didn't carry the warmth of Shabban's greeting, the hiss of his hand-pump, or the laughter of two boys perched on a wooden bench in Valivade, sipping sunshine through glass.

Time flowed forward.

The barracks became houses, the lanes grew quieter,

and Valivade's Gandhinagar Colony blossomed into a permanent, thriving neighborhood.

But memory — like soda — held its sparkle when recalled with love.

When SG thought of those years, it was not the hardship he saw first, but the joy of the sound of corks popping, the gleam of syrup jars in morning light, the laughter of Arjun beside him, and Shabban's voice, warm and gentle, saying, "Fresh batch today, Arjun — best you'll ever have." For in that simple world of brick barracks and soda bubbles, SG had tasted something everlasting — friendship, hope, and the sweet fizz of life beginning again.

Chapter 27

The Line of Dust

The sun sat heavy on the land, burning everything it touched into silence.

A hundred refugees from Sindh stood in a crooked line, clutching paper slips that fluttered like dying leaves.

Dust coated their skin, but not their pride.

Ahead stood a canvas tent—the government relief centre.

Inside, a desk, two chairs, and two clerks.

One slouched with weariness.

The other wore arrogance like a badge.

"You want wheat or rice?" The loud one barked at a frail man.

"Speak up!

I don't have all day." The man trembled over his form.

The clerk chewed something noisily, then spat his contempt into the air.

"These people expect everything to be handed to them," he muttered.

"Charity turns even the proud into beggars." From the line, a voice cracked through the heat—sharp, steady, unmistakable.

"Mind your tongue." Heads turned.

Paari stepped forward.

Her white dupatta gleamed against the dust.

Her hair was pinned neatly, her nose-ring glinted like a spark of rebellion.

Her back was straight; her face calm, carved from the same earth that could not be broken.

"We are not here for your charity," she said evenly.

"We lost our homes, not our self-respect.

You are not doing us a favour by giving what already belongs to the people." The clerk straightened, defensive now.

"You people were running for your lives a month ago. Now you talk like queens?"

Paari's eyes didn't waver.

"Running from fire doesn't make us less than human. Don't mistake displacement for weakness.

You sit there with your rubber stamp and think you're a king.

But remember—you serve the people.

Not rule them." The man slammed his hand on the desk.

"You'd rather starve than take help from the government, is it?"

"Help given with contempt isn't help.

It's poison disguised as kindness." A younger officer entered—his uniform still crisp, his eyes kind but weary.

He stopped, taking in the scene.

"That's enough," he said quietly to the older man.

"If you can't speak with respect, leave.

No one here is beneath you." The rude clerk went silent, shame burning his face.

The young officer turned to Paari and bowed slightly.

"Madam, please accept my apology.

You all deserve dignity." Paari studied him for a long moment.

Then she turned—not to him, but to the women waiting behind her.

"Come," she said.

"Let's go." Someone whispered, "But the rations—"
"We'll find our own food," Paari said.

"But not at the cost of our dignity." She walked away.

The others followed, their heads high.

The line dissolved behind her like a mirage fading in sunlight.

The tent, the clerks, the dust—all stayed still.

Only her white dupatta moved, fluttering like a flag of quiet defiance.

They walked in silence past barracks, past men sitting stunned, past children playing with pebbles instead of toys.

The air smelled of dry earth and loss.

But Paari walked like a woman who remembered purpose.

Every step was steady.

Every gesture deliberate.

At last, she stopped beneath a neem tree.

The women gathered around her, their faces lined with fear, fatigue, and questions.

"Paari," one of them said softly, "what now?

We've left the centre.

How will we eat?

What about the children?" Paari looked at her—not with pity, but with strength.

"We did not cross deserts, bury our dead, and carry our children in our arms just to wait for handouts," she said.

"We are displaced, yes.

But we are not broken.

We are Sindhi women—our hands remember work even when our hearts are tired." She turned, her gaze sweeping over them.

Looking at her daughter-in-law Bhagyavanti, Paari said, "Bhaagi—you make papad better than anyone.

Start again.

Roll them, dry them, sell them in the village nearby."

" Moomal—you sew.

There are hundreds of women here.

Clothes tear, babies grow.

Stitch what they need." The women exchanged uncertain glances.

"Make pickles," Paari continued.

"Grind spices.

Make phulkas for bachelors.

Draw mehendi, teach letters, tell stories.

Do anything.

But do not wait for someone to remember you." Someone whispered, "But who will buy?" Paari smiled slightly.

"We will sell.

To the villagers, to traders.

Let them see—we are not a camp of beggars.

We are a camp of doers." The silence that followed wasn't hopeless anymore.

It was heavy with thought.

Then, slowly, the women began to nod.

A spark.

Small, but alive.

Hope, like dough, only needs warm hands to rise.

Days passed.

The space under the neem tree began to change.

Woven mats lined the ground.

Bhaagi sat with stacks of golden papads tied in string.

Moomal worked on a borrowed sewing machine, the rhythmic hum of the needle like a heartbeat.

Other women ground masalas, their laughter mixing with the scent of roasted jeera.

They called it "The Women's Corner." Soon, it became the centre of the whole camp.

They bartered papads for pickles, masalas for blouses.

They stitched, cooked, taught, created.

No one waited for charity anymore.

Even the men working hard were drawn by the quiet energy that pulsed under the neem tree.

And one day, nearby villagers wandered in—curious, drawn by the scent of frying spices.

"What is all this?" One asked.

Paari, seated in the shade, answered calmly.

"What we know.

What we brought with us.

Nothing borrowed.

Everything earned." They bought small packets that day—half out of curiosity, half out of respect.

But they came back.

And then others came too.

One morning, the young government officer returned.

He stood for a long moment, watching the scene—the colours, the movement, the laughter.

Paari sat at the centre, back straight, her eyes bright, the air around her humming with quiet pride.

He walked up to her.

"You've built something," he said softly.

"Not just work.

A spirit." Paari nodded.

"They only needed to remember who they were." He looked around, humbled.

"You've done more in a week than we've managed in months." Paari's lips curved in a faint smile.

"Rations feed the body.

Work feeds the soul." He nodded slowly.

"We'll support this.

Maybe set up a stall, a fund—" "Only," she interrupted gently, "if it's given with respect.

Not pity." The officer smiled.

"Respect it is." As he left, a breeze stirred.

The smell of spices and dough drifted through the camp.

Women's laughter filled the air.

It wasn't a village yet.

It wasn't a market.

But it was something to build on.

And at the centre of it all sat Paari— a woman who had lost everything, and still refused to bow.

She was the kind of woman time couldn't erase— a traveller from the ashes of one world to the making of another.

Chapter 28

Midnight Rescue

It was 11:00 PM.
Kolhapur was quiet.
Houses dim.
Roads empty.
The world winding down for sleep.
But in one bungalow at Tarabai Park, a phone began to ring.
Not a mobile.
Not a WhatsApp ping.
The old landline—loud, sharp, urgent.
SG answered it.
"Hello?" The voice on the other end trembled.
"SG... it's Gyan Narsinghani.
Sandeep's gone.
Kidnapped.
I need your help." SG's expression changed in an instant.
Sandeep.
Nineteen.
Charming.
Carefree.
Gyan's nephew.
But more than that—a boy who lived like a prince.
New gadgets.
New clothes.

Fast cars.

And around him, a group of boys—four "friends"—who watched, laughed, envied.

He didn't see it.

But jealousy had been simmering.

And now, it had exploded.

They'd kidnapped him.

And vanished.

SG didn't waste a second.

He got ready, stepped out.

Gyan's car screeched into the driveway.

Next stop: Shashi Gajwani's bungalow.

SG's younger brother.

Respected.

Sharp.

Trusted by everyone.

They woke him up.

Told him everything.

Shashi didn't blink.

He picked up the phone and called the police station himself.

"There's a kidnapping.

It's serious.

The boy is untraceable.

Act immediately." By 11:30 PM, the case was in motion.

A complaint was filed.

The inspector on duty was briefed.

But SG had other instincts.

"Let's go to Panhala," he said.

"At midnight?" Gyan asked.

"If they're hiding, it's either there… or too late." They drove fast.

Through the city.
Tarabai Park.
Collector's office.
River Panchganga.
Then the long, quiet road to Panhala, with dense trees on both sides of the road.
Panhala—a hill station of ancient forts and dense forests—lay 20 kilometers ahead.
As they ascended the narrow roads, the world got quieter.
The darkness deeper.
They searched ruins.
Beamed headlights into trees.
Circled the Panhala Fort.
All the while, they called Sandeep's number.
Over.
And over.
"The number you are trying to reach is switched off." Each time, that robotic voice cut through the hope.
It was now 2:00 AM.
Then, a flash of memory.
"Naresh!" Gyan exclaimed.
"My cousin.
He owns a mobile shop." They called.
No answer.
Called again—his wife picked up, sleepy.
"Please... wake him." Naresh came on the line.
Gyan explained everything, fast, frantic.
"Can you trace the mobile's last signal?" "Give me 15 minutes," Naresh said.
"I'll get back." SG and Gyan turned the car around.
Barreling down toward Kolhapur again.
No words.

Just urgency.
The phone rang again.
It was Naresh.
"He's at Kagal Octroi Naka.
That's where the phone last pinged." Back to the police station.
SG rushed in.
"We've got a location.
Kagal.
Alert the police there now!" Wireless sets buzzed.
Sirens were readied.
Orders were sent.
At Kagal Octroi Post, the night was still.
But not for long.
Just as the old Maruti van tried to cruise past the naka, the police waved them down.
"Stop.
Step out." Four boys inside.
They smiled nervously.
Pretended nothing was wrong.
"Sandeep?
No idea where he is." But the police weren't buying it.
A few well-timed slaps—and the truth came pouring out.
"He's in the back... tied up... please don't hit again..." They opened the back door.
And there he was.
Sandeep.
Hands tied.
Gag in his mouth.
Bruised.
Scared.

But alive.

He had been thrown like luggage into the rear seat.

But one thing had remained on—his mobile, in the back pocket of his jeans.

That signal—was his lifeline.

The kidnappers were arrested on the spot.

They'd planned to call the family at dawn and demand ransom.

It was simple.

Greed dressed up as friendship.

But the night turned against them.

As morning broke and sunlight began to touch the city, Gyan held Sandeep close, choking back emotion.

SG stood nearby.

Calm.

Silent.

But deeply relieved.

They drove straight to Shashi Gajwani's house.

"Bhai," Gyan Narsinghani said, "if you hadn't acted fast... if you hadn't made that call..." Shashi just smiled and placed a hand on Gyan's shoulder.

"Family doesn't wait for danger to knock.

We face it together." Later, they returned to the police station—not with panic this time, but gratitude.

They shook hands with the inspector.

Thanked every constable on duty.

"You didn't just do your job tonight," Gyan said, voice heavy with feeling.

"You saved a life." That night began with fear... but ended with courage, instinct, and the power of standing together.

Sandeep would recover.

The four kidnappers would face justice.

And Kolhapur would sleep a little safer.

Because when good people act fast— even the darkest night can end in rescue.

Chapter 29

The Partition

The war in Europe had ended, but another upheaval had just begun.

India, newly independent and partitioned, now bore its own wounds.

From the north-west came waves of weary Sindhi families — Hindu refugees fleeing Karachi, Hyderabad (Sindh), Sukkur and Larkana — carrying bundles of cloth, memories, and stories deeply immersed in loss.

In the township of Valivade, once home to Polish refugees, the old Polish barracks now took in new guests: the Sindhis.

The mango tree still stood at the edge of the village, and the lanes still echoed with children's feet.

But the songs had changed.

The accents were different.

And the markets were about to become the meeting place of two very different Indias.

One bright morning, Paari marched into the market, her dupatta tucked at her waist.

She spotted a heap of bhindi-lady finger-— fresh, slender, green as spring.

" Ghanaa paisa?

How much?" she asked in Sindhi.

The Marathi vendor, Mai Shinde, narrowed her eyes

and replied, "Teen paise paav." Paari blinked. "Paav?" Mai frowned.

"Tumhala samzat naahi? You don't understand?" Neither understood the other's words, but both understood the tone: Too expensive.

Paari held up four fingers.

"Doh paise..Two paisa." Mai Shinde raised three fingers.

"Teen paise..Three paisa." Paari picked up a particularly fat bhendi, held it between two fingers, and said slowly, " Hee moto aahe na halando...it is thick, will not work for me..... ." Then she pointed to the tender ones, made a snipping motion with her hand.

Mai laughed — she couldn't understand a word, but she recognized drama when she saw it.

They haggled, mimed, and finally settled.

Paari walked away with bhindi (okra), grumbling in Sindhi, while Mai muttered in Marathi — but both had a smile tugging at their lips.

As weeks passed, the Sindhi and Marathi women saw each other daily — over onions, coriander, potatoes, and gossip.

Paari once brought a small bowl of saai bhaaji — the Sindhi spinach-lentil dish — and offered it to Mai Shinde.

Mai sniffed it suspiciously, took a bite, and her eyes widened.

"Chhaan!

Masst..Very delicious!" she declared, licking her fingers.

In return, Mai offered bhakri with thecha, the fiery Marathi garlic-chili chutney.

Paari took a nibble and howled, tears streaming down her cheeks.

" Baahi lagi vayi..it's too spicy!" she cried, fanning her mouth.

Mai started laughing, handing her a piece of jaggery.

" Aag laagli navha....kaahi goad khaa...It's fire..too spicy.. now have a piece of jaggery..sweet...!" They didn't understand the words — but they understood the fire, the kindness, and the shared laughter.

One memorable morning, Rajee, Paari's granddaughter, wore a sari for the first time, draped in her mother's Karachi style — with the pallu tucked in front.

She passed the vegetable stall where Sulochana, a teenage Marathi vendor, was stacking tomatoes.

Sulochana pointed at the sari and giggled.

"Arey, he kaay!

Pallu samor kay lavlay?

What's this...why have you tied the sari pallu on the front?" Rajee, confused by the giggle, raised her eyebrows and said, " Assan Sindh mein heean paaeendaa aahyoon.. This is how we wear it in Sindh." Sulochana, who didn't catch a word but recognized the swag, walked around Rajee, inspecting the drape like a fashion critic.

Then she dramatically flipped Rajee's pallu over her shoulder in classic Maharashtrian style and said, "Ata barobar!" — Now it's right!

Rajee looked in a mirror shard at a nearby stall and burst out laughing.

"Okay okay, I look Kolhapuri now!" Sometimes the women would gather under the banyan tree after the market hours.

They would brew chai in an aluminum kettle, pour it into small glasses, and sit on jute sacks.

One afternoon, Usha, a Marathi woman, sang a Lavani tune with quick claps and rhythmic shoulder sways.

The Sindhi women clapped along, then replied with a haunting Sindhi folk song — slow, soulful, a melody shaped by riverbanks and salt flats.

They didn't know the lyrics.

But the music translated.

At one point, Bhagyavanti came hurrying into the market, holding a cloth pouch.

She approached a vendor and blurted, "Loonh khape..want salt!" The vendor, Dinu, mistook it for "mithai" (sweets), and handed her a pile of laddoos.

Bhagyavanti scowled.

"Na na!

Loonh!

Salt!" Sulochana jumped in, mimed sprinkling over food, and finally shouted, "Loonh... mhanje saindhav... Salt..she wants salt!" Bhagyavanti gasped, smiled, and exclaimed, "Ah!

Ah! Saindhav! Meeth!" remembering the Marathi word for rock salt.

They hugged like war buddies who had cracked a code.

Over time, the Marathi and Sindhi women created a language all their own — part-pantomime, part-teasing, full of warmth.

They exchanged recipes, hair oil secrets, even wedding rituals.

When a Sindhi girl got married, the Marathi women danced to dholki beats they barely understood.

When a Marathi boy got engaged, the Sindhi women turned up in glittering salvar kurtas covered with dupattas, bringing rice and laughter.

The fences between their lives blurred.

That old mango tree still stood, its roots deep in Valivade's soil, its leaves rustling in approval.

It had seen Polish hymns, football games, and now — the songs and stories of women from two different cultures, slowly but steadily understanding each other.

And yet, here they were.

Trading brinjals.

Swapping chutneys.

Laughing over chili burns.

Crying over shared memories of what they had lost — and gained.

In the heart of a divided subcontinent, in a village forgotten by maps, these women stitched together a fabric of friendship — not with words, but with food, fire, laughter, and a language all their own.

Epilogue

Beyond the Horizon

Years passed.
The red dust of Valivade still clung to the earth, but the camp itself had changed.

Where once stood dilapidated barracks, there were now modest brick homes, a larger school, even a small clinic.

The people who had arrived as refugees, broken and dispossessed, had built a life—not the one they had lost, but one they could finally call their own.

Bajo, older now, his hair flecked with grey, remained the heart of the community.

He moved with the same restless energy of youth, his voice carried the same quiet conviction that had once led a thousand to march in defiance.

Major Misal had retired from service but chose not to leave.

The camp was his home now, and its people, his family.

He walked its lanes every morning, sharing tea with old friends, visiting the graves of those lost, including Lachhu's.

He never forgot the boy's face—nor the day the camp had risen not in violence, but in unity.

And Kanhaiya—once the small boy clinging to the

hem of his grieving mother's kurta—had become something more than anyone hoped for.

With the help of Bajo, the community, and Major Misal, Kanhaiya stayed in school, studied by candlelight, and earned a college degree and started his own business.

In the Valivade Camp, the children gathered around him wide-eyed, listening to stories of the time when their parents had stood in the streets and changed their fate.

His presence lit a spark in them: that no matter how powerless you begin, you can rise.

Lachhu's parents grew old in peace, with Kanhaiya taking care of them, and surrounded by the community that never abandoned them.

The small memorial beneath the neem tree was tended with care, fresh marigolds laid every week without fail.

Lachhu was gone, but he was not forgotten.

The camp spoke his name with reverence—as the boy who awakened their courage.

And so Valivade endured.

Not merely as a refugee camp, but as a living symbol of resilience.

A place where injustice met resistance.

Where grief was met with equanimity.

Where a murdered boy's younger brother grew up to change the world.

The dust still settled at dusk.

The lanterns still glowed along the narrow lanes.

And the people—forever resilient, forever supportive—stood tall beneath the open sky.

Beyond the horizon, a new future beckoned.

And Valivade walked towards it together.

Finale

As the decades passed, Bajomal Gajwani, and his family — Bhagyavanti, Paari, Parchomal, Bakhat, and Jaadalmal — built not only a livelihood but a legacy.

What began as a small effort to survive in the aftermath of Partition grew into a respected wholesale business in potatoes, onions, and garlic, known across markets for its fairness and reliability.

Through discipline and determination, they transformed uncertainty into opportunity.

Their reputation for integrity and hard work became their most valuable asset, passed naturally to their children, who carried forward the same principles into new professions and modern enterprises.

Education became the cornerstone of the family's progress, ensuring that the next generation would never again face the insecurity their parents once knew.

Though Partition had displaced them from their homeland, it could not displace their values.

They refused to be bound by bitterness or loss.

Instead, they channeled their energy into rebuilding with purpose, finding dignity in labour and satisfaction in honest trade.

In time, the Gajwani family came to symbolize the

quiet strength of those who rebuilt India after its Partition — men and women who endured without complaint, who worked not for recognition but for stability, respect, and family unity.

Looking back, their journey reflects more than the success of one family.

It tells a larger story — of resilience in exile, of hope amid uncertainty, and of the enduring belief that with integrity, effort, and self-belief, even the most painful displacements can lead to new beginnings.

Their lives stand today as a reminder: history may divide lands, but it cannot divide courage.

Black Eagle Books

www.blackeaglebooks.org
info@blackeaglebooks.org

Black Eagle Books, an independent publisher, was founded as a nonprofit organization in April, 2019. It is our mission to connect and engage the Indian diaspora and the world at large with the best of works of world literature published on a collaborative platform, with special emphasis on foregrounding Contemporary Classics and New Writing.

www.ingramcontent.com/pod-product-compliance
Lightning Source LLC
Chambersburg PA
CBHW060609080526
44585CB00013B/741